GUIDE BOOK

FOR THE

TOURIST AND TRAVELER

OVER THE

VALLEY RAILWAY!

GW00402170

Cuyahoga Valley Scenic Railroad passing under the Rt. 82 bridge in Brecksville.
Cuyahoga Valley Scenic Railroad.

GUIDE BOOK

FOR THE

TOURIST AND TRAVELER

OVER THE

VALLEY RAILWAY!

THE SHORT LINE BETWEEN

CLEVELAND, AKRON AND CANTON.

1880.

BY JOHN S. REESE

FACSIMILE EDITION

With a new introduction by Sam Tamburro and Juliet Galonska

Published in cooperation with Cuyahoga Valley National Park
&
Cuyahoga Valley Scenic Railroad

THE KENT STATE UNIVERSITY PRESS
KENT & LONDON

This publication is made possible in part under a grant
from the Ohio & Erie Canal Association.

The publisher wishes to acknowledge
Sherman and Anne Farnham and Eleanor Morris
for their financial support of this publication.

CONTENTS.

ACKNOWLEDGMENTS.

The reprinting of the *Guide Book for the Tourist and Traveler over the Valley Railway!* has been an interesting and rewarding project. And, like any worthwhile project, there are many individuals and organizations that assisted in the process.

We would like to thank the following organizations and individuals for their support of this project: Progress Through Preservation for assisting with the submission of grant applications; Cuyahoga Valley Scenic Railroad (CVSR), especially current President Douglas O. Cooper and staff members Alicia Campolito and Sue Round for their help and enthusiasm for the project; the Ohio & Erie Canal Association (OECA) for providing a grant to assist with the printing of the book; and OECA staff member Jeff Winstel for his review and comments on the introductory text. Former CVSR President Sherman Farnham, Anne Farnham, and Eleanor Morris also provided financial support that made the inclusion of the introduction possible.

We would also like to acknowledge the staff members of Cuyahoga Valley National Park for their reviews, support, and encouragement, including Superintendent John P. Debo, David T. Humphrey, Jennie Vasarhelyi, and Jennifer McMahon. Special thanks to Anthony Gareau and Ralph Wagnitz for creating the book's maps.

We are also grateful for the assistance of the University of Akron's Archives for allowing us to use their original copy of the *Guide Book for the Tourist and Traveler over the Valley Railway!* to produce the reprint.

We have also benefited from the insights of several other individuals. Both Randolph S. Bergdorf of the Peninsula Library and Historical Society and Michael J. Kole of the Midwest Railway Preservation Society provided sound historical information on the history of the Valley Railway. And Lori Tamburro provided editorial assistance and was instrumental in compiling the book's index.

Finally, we would like to thank Will Underwood and Joanna Hildebrand Craig of The Kent State University Press for their interest in the project and patience during the publication process.

INTRODUCTION.

BY SAM TAMBURRO & JULIET GALONSKA.

The histories for leisure travel and transportation are inextricably linked. The construction of the Valley Railway in 1880 coincided with a growing interest in travel and tourism in the United States. Although touring activity began in the United States as early as the 1820s, it was not until the late nineteenth century that tourism evolved from an elite activity into a mass phenomenon. The middle class that emerged in urban, commercial, and industrial centers had disposable income and leisure time to travel. As railroad fares fell and urban populations increased, more and more people became interested in excursions as a form of revitalization. At the same time that disposable income and expanded leisure time made getaways possible, those operating tourist attractions became more consumer savvy. Commercialism increased as promoters found new ways to sell spectacular scenery or exciting experiences.

The emerging middle class took advantage of the ease of transportation provided by the railroads. The rail companies already had a history of promoting tourism in specific regions of the country. This expanded in the 1880s and 1890s, especially in the West where companies like the Southern Pacific Railroad and the Atchison, Topeka & Santa Fe Railway undertook aggressive campaigns to bring visitors to spectacular scenery in Yosemite and the Grand Canyon. Railroad lines expected to profit from establishment of parks as resort areas and therefore promoted scenic preservation and aided the establishment of such wilderness refuges. Indeed, Jay Cooke and the Northern Pacific Railroad were heavily involved in the creation of Yellowstone as America's first National Park. Once securing a monopoly over transportation to these remote areas, railroads then became active in providing visitor services. They financed the construction of hotels like Old Faithful (1904) and the El Tovar (1905) and published guide books beginning with *Northern Pacific Railroad: The Wonderland Route to the Pacific Coast* in 1885.

It was in this spirit of boosterism that John S. Reese wrote his guide book. Although none of the destination stops were as scenic as Yellowstone National

Valley Railway locomotive engine in the Cleveland rail yard, circa 1887.
Ohio Historical Society.

Park or the Grand Canyon, the Valley Railway's riders could enjoy long stretches of rural scenes connecting the cities of Cleveland, Akron, and Canton. Valley Railway excursions provided an alternative to the pace of life and industrialization of a metropolis like Cleveland (the eleventh largest U.S. city in 1880) and the smaller cities of Akron (population 18,000 in 1880) and Canton (population 12,000 in 1880). Recreation, leisure, contemplation, and appreciation of landscape became part of the emerging middle class's collective consciousness.

"What kind of place is this?" Passengers on the Valley Railway may have well asked themselves that question as they pulled into a station or passed through the countryside. Reese hoped to satisfy their curiosity with his 1880 *Guide Book for the Tourist and Traveler over the Valley Railway!* The paperback publication, which sold for 25 cents, promised "a complete description of the scenery and objects of interest along the road." For passengers who spent hours peering out the windows, the guide book was certainly a welcome companion. The role, if any, of the Valley Railway in the production of the guide book is not known. Reese is listed as the compiler and publisher of the work, and nowhere in the text is the Valley Railway Company acknowledged as a sponsor of the guide.

The Preface provides much information about the preparation of Reese's guide book. According to Reese, he began the project in May 1880 and completed the book by July. And, if we are to believe Reese, he compiled the guide book by walking the entire fifty-seven-mile line in ninety-degree temperatures in order to have all of the facts complete and correct. Interestingly, only roughly a quarter of the book's text is devoted to landscape descriptions of the Valley Railway. Nearly half of Reese's guide book is devoted to local advertisements from Cleveland, Akron, Canton, and communities in between. The advertisements range from the Aultman Company's Buckeye Reapers to local banks and bookshops. Reese does not indicate if the book's production costs were financed through advertisements, but that would have been characteristic of other local "civic" publications.

Reese is also given to hyperbole in the book's Preface, claiming that the "work [is] different from anything that has ever been published in this or any other country." In reality, railroad travel guides were common by the 1850s. In fact, a guide book for Ohio's railroads, entitled *The Ohio Railroad Guide, Illustrated: Cincinnati to Erie Via Columbus and Cleveland,* was published in 1854. As a genre, travel guides and journals developed along with railroads and were often sponsored by the railroad companies themselves.

Many of the late-nineteenth-century railroad guide books, including Reese's, also focused on the man-made environment, especially the engineering marvels built by the railroad companies. The infrastructure created for the railroads–bridges, viaducts, trestles, and roadbeds–were illustrated in lithographs to demonstrate man's control of nature and environment. In Reese's guide book, several of the illustrations center on the Valley Railway's engineering "feats," many of which are still evident in the cultural landscape today.

Naturally, railroad guide books emphasized landscape features in plain view from the train, such as long-range vistas of mountain ranges, deserts, and rock formations. Even within the limited miles between Cleveland and Canton, Reese found interesting landscape elements to identify, such as the Brecksville Rock outcropping and the bottom lands of the Cuyahoga River Valley.

Similar to Reese's focus on the natural landscape, the Valley Railway Company's advertisements also reflect a focus on the scenic nature of the line and its recreational potential. An 1884 Valley Railway advertisement announced that "We have the finest picnic grounds in the state" at Cuyahoga Falls, Gaylord's Grove, Silver Lake, and Zoar. In 1888, Zoar, Myers' Lake, and Cottage Grove Lake were proclaimed the finest "excursion grounds" in the state. The advertisement continued that at the newly opened Cottage Grove resort, "no pains have been spared to make this charming retreat the most attractive, select and enjoyable of all watering places." The Cleveland Terminal & Valley Railroad, a successor to the Valley Railway, continued the tradition, making a point of announcing that there were three trains traveling between Akron, Canton, and Cleveland on Sundays, promoting the line's recreational "day-trip" potential.

Although Reese's intent in the book was clear, his private life has proved to be less lucid. John S. Reese, of Canton, is a historical specter who has slipped into the shadows of the past, leaving little evidence of his existence beyond the guide book. To date, we have not been able to locate any of Reese's relatives who have knowledge of his history. He also escaped the watchful eye of the U.S. Census Bureau, not appearing in any of Canton's census reports for that period. Other obvious sources, such as newspapers, marriage records, and obituaries, have led to few historical clues. Reese does, however, appear in the *Canton, Ohio Directory* during the late nineteenth century.

In 1881, a year after the guide book was published, Reese's occupation is listed as a painter with a residence on West Tuscarawas Avenue. Throughout the 1880s, the entries in the city directory for John S. Reese reveal that he maintained a transient lifestyle, changing occupations and residences often. During the 1880s, he is listed at nine different addresses and held numerous occupations including painter, milk peddler, clerk for the Valley Railway, and finally printer. By 1893, he appears to have married a woman named Frances. It is not known if the couple had any children. After 1899, Reese no longer appears in the city directory; however, Frances continues to be listed for several additional years. He does not show up in any of Stark County's death records, and Frances is not listed as a widow in the directories after 1899, which was customary. If Reese left Canton, where he moved is unknown.

It would have been hard for John S. Reese to imagine that an audience would still be interested in his guide book more than a century after it had been originally published. However, Reese's work is indeed still relevant to twenty-first-century readers. Originally produced to spur interest and develop a passenger base for the Valley Railway, the book's descriptions of the railroad's views and vistas and community histories serve as snapshots of the 1880 environment and culture.

Also, with its abundant advertisements for local businesses, the book is an expression of the regional economy that thrived during that period. However, the book lacks a historical context. Because he was writing in the initial year of its operation, Reese was unable to capture the history and heritage of the Valley Railway. Reese could only imagine the impact the railroad would have on the communities it served. In the pages that follow, we try to fill in the historical blanks left by the *Guide Book for the Tourist and Traveler over the Valley Railway!* The corporate history of the Valley Railway proved to be brief, lasting approximately twenty years; however, the lasting impact of the line, especially in rural areas, was significant. The Valley Railway represented a regional "metropolitan corridor," tying together three cities and several communities in Northeast Ohio. Today, in fact, the Cuyahoga Valley Scenic Railroad travels on much the same grade as its historic predecessor, and, again, those communities are linked by a local rail line.

In the aftermath of the War of 1812, the State of Ohio pursued the development of internal improvements to link its burgeoning agricultural economy to the eastern seaboard. With the opening of New York's Erie Canal in 1825, Ohio began the construction of the Ohio & Erie (O&E) Canal. With the completion of the O&E Canal in 1832, both the Cuyahoga Valley and Tuscarawas Valley entered into the transportation era. The O&E Canal connected the Great Lakes watershed with the Mississippi watershed, dramatically increasing the speed and quantity of agricultural goods brought to market. The predominance of the canal age only lasted approximately thirty years; by the 1860s, railroads emerged as a more efficient mode of transportation to market. Railroads did not depend on water sources, such as rivers, and could operate year around, relatively unaffected by floods and freezing temperatures.

The decade of the 1850s remains one of the most dynamic eras in American railroad development. By the mid-1850s, the United States, with around 5 percent of the world's population, had nearly as much railroad mileage as the rest of

Botzum Depot with passengers awaiting a train on the platform, circa 1896.
Cuyahoga Valley National Park.

the world combined. The State of Ohio also experienced its first large-scale railroad construction during the 1850s. For example, in 1850 Ohio maintained 500 miles of railroad track. By 1860, the number had soared to 3,000 miles–the most in the nation. The railroad companies sought direct access to the coal fields of the Mahoning and Tuscarawas Valleys, a shipping lane previously controlled by the Ohio canal system. In Northeast Ohio, mainline railroad tracks followed either an east-west axis or a southeast-southwest diagonal.

Completed in February 1851, the Cleveland, Columbus & Cincinnati Railroad became the first Cleveland railroad line. In 1852, the Cleveland & Pittsburgh Railroad opened, running east of the Cuyahoga Valley through Hudson, Ohio. By 1851, the Cleveland, Painesville & Eastern Railroad opened and served as the area's east-west link to cities such as Erie, Pennsylvania, and Buffalo, New York. With the exception of the Cleveland & Pittsburgh Railroad, the Cuyahoga Valley remained excluded from early railroad development. Despite organized efforts to route a railroad directly through the Cuyahoga Valley during the 1850s, the valley would endure without rail service until the 1880s.

As early as 1830, with the planned construction of the Clinton Line Railroad (CLRR), the Cuyahoga Valley entertained plans for a railroad. Proposed by New York's De Witt Clinton Jr., the CLRR would stretch from New York City to Council Bluffs, Iowa, and would traverse the southern section of the valley (Summit County) along the east-west axis. By 1853, with sufficient capital available, track preparation began in the five states through which the CLRR would pass. The CLRR organized a board of directors for the "Extension," the line between Hudson and Tiffin, with Professor Henry Day of Hudson as its president. However, financial support for the CLRR slowly declined, and by 1856 the board of directors halted construction of the Extension line indefinitely. That same year, the CLRR claimed bankruptcy, and investors in Hudson lost their stockholdings. The push for rail service in the Cuyahoga Valley continued, but it took an additional twenty-four years before it became a reality.

The founding of the Valley Railway came in the late 1860s when a group of regional entrepreneurs from Cleveland, Akron, and Canton organized to form the Valley Railway. Akron's David L. King proved to be a key figure in the creation of the Valley Railway. Harvard educated, King practiced law in Akron and founded the law firm King & King with his brother in 1849. He also served as the executor of his deceased father's landed estate. King was professionally associated with the Akron Sewer Pipe Company, a company that would be eventually served by the Valley Railway. King also founded the King Varnish Company, but the company was fraught with financial problems and ended in bankruptcy in 1888. Probably one of his most enduring business arrangements was the Valley Railway.

Edwin Bell Howe at the Hawkins Depot, circa 1890s. The Hawkins Depot was renamed "Ira" to avoid confusion with another stop on the B&O Railroad. *Cuyahoga Valley National Park.*

In 1869, King secured a charter for the Akron & Canton Railway, which officially became the Valley Railway on August 21, 1871. The proposed Valley Railway would parallel the Cuyahoga River Valley, stretching from southeast Cleveland to Akron and then on to Canton and Valley Junction in Tuscarawas County. Even though the City of Canton's first railroad line, the Ohio & Pennsylvania Railroad, opened in 1852, the city would not be connected to Cleveland until 1880 with the opening of the Valley Railway.

King originally owned a significant amount of stock in the Cleveland, Zanesville & Cincinnati Railroad and realized the financial potential of linking the rich coal fields of Stark and Tuscarawas Counties with the industrial centers of Akron and Cleveland. To establish customers for his freight and gain financial support, King sought counsel and aid from Cleveland, Akron, and Canton industrialists.

In Cleveland, King recruited the assistance of several of the city's leading businessmen, such as Nathan Payne, Stillman Witt, and Sylvester T. Everett, to serve as officers for the railway. In 1860, Nathan Payne, a lifelong resident of Cleveland, became a partner in the coal company Cross, Payne & Company, which later became Payne, Newton & Company. He was also involved in local politics, serving two terms on the local board of education and six years on city council several times between 1862 and 1872. He was elected mayor of Cleveland on the Democratic ticket in 1875 but served only one term. He declined renomination because of the conflict of interest with his business activities, especially his involvement with the Valley Railway.

Stillman Witt, a long-time railroad man, was another logical choice for involvement with the creation of the Valley Railway. Witt served as one of the principals of Harbach, Stone & Witt, a railroad construction company responsible for building the Cleveland, Columbus & Cincinnati Railroad; the Cleveland, Painesville, & Ashtabula Railroad; and the Cleveland & Newburg Railroad. Witt was also one of the founders of the Cleveland Rolling Mill Company, a company that would become an important customer of the Valley Railway. Unfortunately, Witt died in 1875, never seeing the completion of the Valley Railway line in 1880. Sylvester T. Everett, vice president and treasurer of the Valley Railway, was in the banking business and served as Cleveland's city treasurer between 1869 and 1883. Standard Oil's Henry Flagler and Cleveland Rolling Mill's A. B. Stone also served on the Valley Railway board of directors.

The leadership of the Valley Railway through the 1870s and 1880s also reflected the business leadership in Canton. Board member James A. Saxton was the founder of the Stark County Bank. Member George Cook was the director of Aultman Miller and Company, a manufacturer of reapers and mowers, and also served on the board of the First National Bank in Akron. Member James Farmer, earlier involved in the founding of the Cleveland & Pittsburgh Railroad, was president of the Ohio National Bank.

When the Valley Railway finally began service in 1880, it immediately achieved the goal of filling the void in local service to Cleveland, Akron, and Canton. Although each of these cities was served by other rail lines by that date, no other railroad passed through the Cuyahoga Valley and provided direct access to the coal fields in Stark and Tuscarawas Counties.

King clearly defined the Valley Railway's objective–to carry passengers south from Cleveland to Akron and Canton and return with coal from the south. He concluded that the downhill grade from Akron to Cleveland allowed for the transportation of an increased tonnage of coal. The route from Cleveland through Akron to Canton contained low grades and wide curves perfect for hauling bulk shipments of raw resources. King and his advisers realized that the growing industries of Cleveland, especially the iron mills, would demand even larger amounts of coal to fuel their operations. They were also aware that the Mahoning Valley coal fields near Youngstown, Ohio, which supplied Cleveland at that time, were rapidly depleting. King still had two more critical decisions to make: how to finance the Valley Railway and what the track gauge size should be.

Similar to most nineteenth-century railroad ventures, the Valley Railway attempted to raise capital through the sale of company stock. King chose committeemen from each of the counties through which the Valley Railway would pass, and stock subscriptions opened at Cleveland, Akron, Canton, and intermediate points in January 1872. The Valley Railway committeemen expected Cleveland to raise $500,000 and Akron and Canton to raise $150,000 each. Intermediate points were assigned proportional shares. First Canton, then Akron, reached full-share, but Cleveland proved to be ineffectual at raising the capital.

The Valley Railway's route into Cleveland followed the Cuyahoga River Flats in the bed of the abandoned Ohio & Erie Canal. In 1874, after much debate, Cleveland City Council signed a deal with the newly formed Valley Railway to lease the former canal bed to the railroad for a period of ninety-nine years. For payment, the city received $265,000 of Valley Railway bonds. As construction on the Valley Railway began, the canal bed was filled with rail ballast to hold tracks. The city eventually met their $500,000 pledge by voluntary subscriptions to the railroad's capital stock.

Gauge size became another problematic issue for the Valley Railway. After the Civil War, increasing numbers of railroad companies standardized their track size from 3 feet to 4 feet 8.5 inches. The Baltimore & Ohio, the Pennsylvania, and the New York Central Railroads all adopted the standard gauge. If the Valley Railway chose to install standard gauge, the upshot would be twofold: easier connections with national railroad companies and increased tonnage capacity per railcar. The downside would be cost. Although the narrow gauge represented minimal construction costs, David L. King and the other officers of the Valley Railway opted for the more expensive standard gauge in hopes of future benefits.

The biggest problem facing the Valley Railway concerned the construction and funding of the railroad. On February 3, 1873, the Valley Railway awarded a construction contract for the entire line to Akron's Nicholas E. Vansickle and Arthur L. Conger, and within a month they broke ground in Springfield Township, Summit County. Disagreements between the Valley Railway's directors and Vansickle & Conger were frequent, and on May 16, 1874, the construction contract ended abruptly, bringing work on the railway to a halt. Construction of the valley line would remain dormant for four more years while the board of directors sought additional capital and another contractor to build the railway.

The domestic market for the Valley Railway stock eroded with the collapse of New York financial firm Jay Cooke and Company, which all but ended eastern loans to most new railroad enterprises. Without an alternative, David L. King personally assumed the entire $150,000 of the Valley Railway's financial liabilities and focused his hopes on English capitalists for additional funds. In February

1875, King visited England to solicit the sale of company securities to a number of London's financiers. Unfortunately for King, news of the Wabash & Western Railroad bankruptcy reached London and caused the British House of Commons to discredit the value of American securities entirely. King left Britain empty handed.

Even though the Valley Railway lacked sufficient capital funds, on August 7, 1878, construction resumed with a new contracting firm, Walsh and Moynahan. In October, King ceremoniously laid the first rail near Akron's Old Forge, but problems soon arose between the contracting firm and the board of directors. Unsatisfied with Walsh and Moynahan's performance and quality of work, the board of directors annulled their contract in January 1879. The contracting firm of Strong and Cary eventually completed the Valley Railway in the winter of 1879–80, and the fifty-seven miles of track from Cleveland to Canton officially opened.

In 1882, the Valley Railway extended a line twenty-six miles south of Canton to Valley Junction in Tuscarawas County, thereby permitting direct connections to the Wheeling & Lake Erie Railroad and the Cleveland & Marietta Railroad. By 1891, the Valley Railway contained seventy-five miles of mainline track, nineteen miles of branch track, and thirty-five miles of side track. In the initial year of operation, the Valley Railway maintained sixteen depots, all of which are identified in Reese's guide book. Within the Cuyahoga Valley, the communities that served as depot stops were Independence, Brecksville, Boston, Peninsula, Everett, Ira (Hawkins), and Botzum. The Valley Railway constructed additional spur lines to the Independence Stone Quarry, F. Schumacher's quarries, and Lawson Waterman's quarries near Peninsula, Boston Mills, and the Jaite Paper Mill.

During the first decade of its operation, the Valley Railway's main cargoes were bulk goods, such as coal, stone, iron, copper, sand, lime, and ore. A spur line connected the Valley Railway with the quarries, and the railroad served as an important transportation link to the Peninsula stone quarries. The quarries of Lawson Waterman employed as many as two hundred men and served as the village's primary industry. Although the Valley Railway had success transporting stone products, it faced constant competition from the Ohio & Erie Canal to ship the Cuyahoga Valley's agricultural goods. As a result, profits from transporting farm products made up only a small portion of the line's total revenue.

The Valley Railway also served as an important transportation link between two burgeoning metropolitan areas: Akron and Cleveland. Akron appears to have been the base of the passenger operation for the Valley Railway. Originally, the Valley Railway's line ran north of the city. However in 1884, the City of Akron granted the Valley Railway permission to extend a spur line directly into the heart of the city. In 1887, the Valley Railway Company built a large passenger depot on the corner of Canal and West Market Streets, a symbol of its presence in Akron. The 1888 statistics for passenger service indicate that most traffic flowed south to north. For that year, Akron recorded 78,586 departures compared with Cleveland's 58,632. By the late 1880s, four trains ran daily each way between Cleveland and Valley Junction, and one additional train serviced Akron and Cleveland. In the Cuyahoga Valley, Peninsula proved to be the busiest depot, with 8,309 departures, followed by Botzum (4,001), Everett (2,981), Independence (2,770), Boston (2,717), Ira (1,731), and Tinker's Creek (1,082).

Railroad depots became hubs of activity for the towns they served. Telegraph service and mail delivery emanated from depots. Travelers to and from the community congregated there. In many ways, the depot functioned as a gateway to the larger world. Businesses, often dependent on train transportation, also developed near depots. The arrival of railroads in a town also meant that different types of business activity could take place. In Boston, a village founded in 1806 and a center for canal boat building, the presence of the Valley Railway line helped to promote the opening of the Cleveland-Akron Bag Company in 1900. Within a few years, the company owned approximately two hundred acres and constructed

Valley Railway Passenger Depot in Akron, completed in 1887.
University of Akron Archives.

a general store and company houses to house the Polish immigrants employed there. A similar enterprise resulted in the founding of Jaite (formerly known as Vaughn) approximately two miles north of Boston. In 1905, the Jaite Paper Mill Company opened a facility and built a store and housing for employees.

The presence of depots was not the only tangible evidence of the railroad's impact. Even before the first trains ran along the Valley Railway line, residents of local communities saw changes to their environment. Construction crews moved and leveled earth. Long lines of parallel wooden ties served as support for steel tracks. The task of extracting gravel, necessary for stabilizing the roadbed, from nearby quarries took on new urgency. Stations and platforms soon appeared alongside the tracks.

These physical intrusions on the landscape also represented the enormous influence railroad companies wielded over community life that traditionally was

Travelers on the Valley Railway await a train at the Boston Mill Depot, circa 1890s.
Western Reserve Historical Society.

Boston Mill Depot, 1910. *Cuyahoga Valley National Park.*

shaped by local concerns. Architecture was usually standardized, as was time-keeping. Indeed, in 1883, the railroads were responsible for creating four separate "time zones" in the United States in order to keep schedules and avoid wrecks. Time was no longer kept on a local basis. Officials of railroad companies, often making decisions far removed from local communities, determined the routes, fares, and schedules. Sometimes, even the names of places along the line reflected the impact of the railroad. In the Cuyahoga Valley, the community of Unionville was renamed Everett in honor of Sylvester T. Everett, vice president and treasurer of the Valley Railway.

Despite its apparent diversity, financial problems and consistent competition from the Connotton Valley Railroad (CVRR) plagued the Valley Railway. The CVRR began operations in 1882 and serviced a route similar to the Valley Railway, stretching from Cleveland's industrial flats district to the coal fields of Tuscarawas County. By 1888, the movement of freight accounted for more than 75 percent of the Valley Railway's total income. Coal constituted nearly 44 percent of the total freight tonnage hauled, while agricultural products contributed

Peninsula Depot and Freight House, circa 1890. *Peninsula Library & Historical Society.*

less than 6 percent to the company's tonnage. The opening of the CVRR resulted in diminished freight tonnage for the Valley Railway, which added to the
company's financial woes.

The Valley Railway also experienced significant losses in passenger service.
As noted earlier, passenger traffic on the road remained largely local. Although it
provided passenger service to Washington, D.C., and Chicago through its connection with the Baltimore & Ohio (B&O) Railroad, the Valley Railway became
the primary route from Akron to Cleveland and valley points in between. Local
traffic, especially from Akron and Cleveland, deteriorated after the completion of
the Northern Ohio Interurban Railroad between these termini in 1895.

In 1890, the B&O acquired a controlling interest in the Valley Railway, thereby
using it to gain important access to the Port of Cleveland. Sylvester T. Everett,
former treasurer, became the vice president of the Valley Railway, and Thomas
M. King, a B&O official in Baltimore, held the presidency. During the early 1890s,
the U.S. economy suffered a severe depression that affected many railroad companies, including the Valley Railway. The Valley Railway fell into receivership in
1892 and eventually declared bankruptcy in 1895. A reorganized company, the

Cleveland Terminal & Valley (CT&V) Railroad, also under the control of the B&O, acquired the Valley Railway's assets in 1895 and began to make improvements to the system. Most of the major enhancements to the line occurred in the Cleveland area, which included a new passenger depot at Canal and Columbus Roads and a new roundhouse on West 3rd Street. The CT&V provided one of Cleveland's most direct rail links with Washington, D.C. As a result, government officials and politicians frequently used the new depot.

By 1915, the CT&V had come under the complete control of the B&O, and by the 1920s traffic on the railroad began to decline as new forms of transportation, such as automobiles and buses, provided competition. By the 1920s, automobiles minimized the use of trains for passenger service. The number of private automobiles registered in the United States increased from 8,000 in 1900 to 8 million in 1920 and 23 million in 1930. Rising in tandem with the increase in auto ownership, the mileage of surfaced highways doubled between 1921 and 1930 and again between 1930 and 1940. "Compared to travel by railroad," notes author John Jakle, "touring by automobile offered freedom of action, closer contact with place, and novel kinds of sociability." No longer was one dependent on a

Baltimore & Ohio Railroad arriving at Jaite Station, circa 1950.
Cuyahoga Valley National Park.

Clara Sager using the Mail
Crane at the Everett Station,
circa 1925. *Peninsula Library
& Historical Society.*

schedule and route determined by the railroad company. Route traffic was re-
vived briefly during World War II but continued to decline steadily afterward.
Still, limited passenger travel on the former Valley Railway line continued in the
first half of the twentieth century before ceasing entirely in 1962.

The Valley Railway's freight traffic suffered a similar fate. In the twentieth century trucks became the chief means of transportation of the valley's products. In
1962–63, the Chesapeake & Ohio (C&O) Railroad purchased the B&O, and the
Valley Railway became part of the C&O, or Chessie System. The corporate railroad
mergers and acquisitions continued, and eventually the Chessie System merged
with Seaboard Coast Line to become CSX Transportation Corporation in 1980.

In the mid-1970s, the Cuyahoga Valley Preservation and Scenic Railway Association (CVPSR) began offering train excursions through the newly formed
Cuyahoga Valley National Recreation Area (CVNRA) on what was known as
the Cuyahoga Valley Line (CVL). Using a Light Mikado steam engine, No. 4070,

the last operating steam engine of its type in the world, and cars provided by the Midwest Railway Historical Foundation, the CVPSR organized routes that ran from the Cleveland Zoo to Hale Farm & Village and then to Quaker Square in Akron before making the return trip to Cleveland. CSX abandoned twenty-six miles of rail line through the Cuyahoga Valley in 1985, and a 1986 federal law provided for the acquisition of twenty-six miles of the rail corridor through CVNRA. No trains ran on the line in 1986 or 1987. In 1987, the National Park Service paid $2.5 million to purchase the track, and excursion trains have run on the line since 1988. Originally the CVL was a steam-engine excursion line, but because of costs and maintenance, the line switched to diesel engines in 1991.

CVL reorganized as Cuyahoga Valley Scenic Railroad (CVSR) in 1994. Today the line continues the tradition of tourism and recreation through Cuyahoga Valley National Park, the designation of National Recreation Area having been

Present-day Peninsula Depot with the Cuyahoga Valley Scenic Railroad in the foreground. *Cuyahoga Valley Scenic Railroad.*

changed in October 2000. While the scenery remains a prime attraction, passengers also enjoy links to the Towpath Trail, local museums, and unique shopping areas. CVSR services have continued to expand with the acquisition of equipment, including locomotives dating from the 1950s and the luxurious passenger car Saint Lucie Sound, as well as the expansion of special programs. Education has become a focus with "Student Explorer" trips highlighting the cultural and natural heritage of the Cuyahoga Valley. CVSR also hosts the annual Polar Express, a fantasy trip to the North Pole based on Chris Van Allsburg's children's book of the same name, and various special events and fund raisers throughout the year. The National Park Service's commitment to the railroad continues. The most recent efforts have resulted in the 2001 opening of the Peninsula Depot Visitor Center in a historic Valley Railway Combination Station, as well as the construction of boarding stations at Brecksville, Boston Mill, Indigo Lake, and Northside in downtown Akron. Additional boarding sites are planned for Canton, Rockside Road, Hillside Road, and Botzum.

Perhaps the largest initiative for the NPS and CVSR is the extension of rail service from Akron into Canton and from Rockside Road, at the national park's north boundary, into downtown Cleveland. Service to downtown Canton is expected to begin in the summer of 2003, with Cleveland service anticipated by 2005. While discussions about such expansion periodically arose since the early 1980s, it was the 1996 designation of the Ohio & Erie Canal National Heritage Corridor that spurred momentum. This heritage area, one of twenty-three with national status in the United States, is a 110-mile corridor extending from Cleveland to New Philadelphia. This multipartner effort, which extends through Cuyahoga, Summit, Stark, and Tuscarawas Counties, includes federal, state, regional, and local government entities; historical societies; nonprofit organizations; businesses; and others. The intent of the Corridor is to help local entities protect and use historic, cultural, and recreational resources for community benefit and economic development while raising regional and national awareness of their unique importance. As identified in the management plan for the Corridor, CVSR is one of three "journey networks" that guide visitors through this area and assist with their discovery of the resources. The other linear features are the multipurpose Towpath Trail, first opened in 1993, running along the Ohio & Erie Canal bed and the CanalWay Ohio National Scenic Byway established in 2000.

There is a rich and interesting history surrounding the Valley Railway and the *Guide Book for the Tourist and Traveler over the Valley Railway!* The author, John S. Reese, remains a historical enigma, escaping out of the public sphere shortly after the publication of his guide book. The book was just as ephemeral as Reese. Printed as a paperback, few of the original copies of the guide book still exist.

The Valley Railway Company also proved to be short-lived. Beginning with fits and starts in the early 1870s and ending in bankruptcy in 1895, the Valley Railway was a symbol of a local enterprise with a regional vision. As you page through the reprinted guide book, you will have a sense of the 1880 environment in which the Valley Railway functioned as well as the history and heritage that the Cuyahoga Valley Scenic Railroad interprets today. Enjoy your trip on the Valley Railway!

SELECTED BIBLIOGRAPHY

Baltimore & Ohio Railroad Standard Plans for Maintenance of Way and Construction. 1907. Reprint. Akron: Akron Railroad Club, 1977.

Brown, Dona. *Inventing New England: Regional Tourism in the Nineteenth Century.* Washington, D.C.: Smithsonian Institution Press, 1995.

Grabowski, John J. "The Valley Line: Pastoral but Practical." *Western Reserve Historical Society News* (July/August 1982): 46–49.

Grismer, Karl H. *Akron and Summit County.* Akron: Summit County Historical Society, 1957.

Jakle, John. *The Tourist: Travel in Twentieth-Century North America.* Lincoln: University of Nebraska Press, 1985.

Kammen, Michael. *Mystic Chords of Memory: The Transformation of Tradition in American Culture.* New York: Knopf, 1991.

Kasson, John. *Civilizing the Machine: Technology and Republican Values in America, 1776–1900.* New York: Grossman, 1976.

Lane, Samuel A. *Fifty Years and Over of Akron and Summit County.* Akron: Beacon Job Department, 1892.

Marx, Leo. *The Machine in the Garden: Technology and the Pastoral Ideal in America.* New York: Oxford University Press, 1964.

Mould, David H. *Dividing Lines: Canals, Railroads and Urban Rivalry in Ohio's Hocking Valley, 1825–1875.* Dayton: Wright State University Press, 1994.

Ninth Annual Report of the Board of Directors of the Valley Railway Company of Ohio to the Stockholders for the Year Ending December 31, 1888. Cleveland, 1889.

Noble, Allen G. "Small Towns." *A Geography of Ohio.* Ed. Leonard Peacefull. Kent: Kent State University Press, 1996. 211–21.

Paris, Jay. "The Saga of Engine 4070." *Historic Preservation* 8.1 (1985): 23–27.

Perrin, William H. *History of Summit County.* Chicago: Baskin and Battey, 1881.

Pomeroy, Earl. *In Search of the Golden West: The Tourist in Western America.* New York: Knopf, 1957.

Poor's Manual of Railroads. New York: H. V. & H. W. Poor, 1880–90.

Runte, Alfred. *Trains of Discovery: Western Railroads and the National Parks.* Boulder & Flagstaff: Northland Press, 1984.

Schlereth, Thomas J. *Victorian American: Transformations in Everyday Life, 1876–1915.* New York: Harper Collins, 1991.

Scrattish, Nick. *Historic Resource Study: Cuyahoga Valley National Recreation Area.* Denver: National Park Service, 1985.

Sears, John F. *Sacred Places: American Tourist Attractions in the Nineteenth Century.* New York: Oxford University Press, 1989.

Stilgoe, John R. *Metropolitan Corridor: Railroads and the American Scene.* New Haven: Yale University Press, 1983.

Ward, James. *Railroads and the Character of America, 1820–1887.* Knoxville: University of Tennessee Press, 1986.

Great Trestle near Akron.—(See pages 16 and 30.)

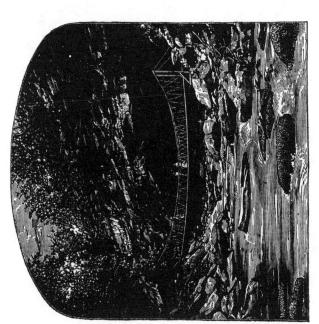

Views in High Bride Glens.—(See page 95.)

GUIDE BOOK

FOR THE

TOURIST AND TRAVELER

OVER THE

VALLEY RAILWAY!

THE SHORT LINE BETWEEN

CLEVELAND, AKRON AND CANTON.

1880.

CONTAINING A COMPLETE DESCRIPTION OF THE SCENERY AND OBJECTS OF
INTEREST ALONG THE ROAD; HISTORY OF EACH STATION
ON THE LINE; BIOGRAPHIES OF THE OFFI-
CERS OF THE ROAD, ETC.

PRICE 25 CENTS.

JOHN S. REESE,

Compiler and Publisher,

CANTON, OHIO.

CANTON, O,
C. C. THOMPSON, PRINTER,
1880.

CONTENTS.

ILLUSTRATIONS.

PREFACE.

"It is done"—the long-looked for VALLEY RAILWAY GUIDE BOOK is before you. After laboring four months under many disadvantages and encountering various misfortunes, we are able to place before the public the present volume which we hope will merit the approval of all.

The object of this book is to familiarize the traveler and tourist with the country they are passing through, and to give an idea of what kind of a place each station is. A person as they are riding along, and pass a factory or particular point of interest will often ask, "What kind of a factory is that, or what do they manufacture there?" or as they come into a station will ask, "What kind of a place is this?" This book fully explains everything to be seen on the VALLEY RAILWAY, and tells you what kind of a place each station is. Refer to this book for a description of everything to be seen from the cars, and for the history of each station. See index.

The work of compiling this book was commenced on the 10th of May last, and everything was ready for the printer by July 10th, but on account of various delays on the part of the printer, it was impossible to have it appear before now. During the second week in May a photographing wagon was taken over the line and prominent points photographed and sent to the engravers at Cleveland. Most of the engravings were executed by Messrs. Murray & Heiss, whose superior work can be seen at a glance.

All the work on this book has been done by the compiler except the engraving, printing, and the help of an advertising solicitor for one week. In order to have everything correct and complete, it was necessary to travel the entire length of the line on foot, which was done by the compiler during the month of June, when the thermometer averaged 90 deg. in the shade. To travel on foot all day, stopping occasionally to make inquiries or take notes, was no easy task. We have, as the result of our labor, produced a work different from anything that has ever been published in this or any other country.

We feel indebted to many persons along the road who have lent us their aid in making this book a success. For our history of Cleveland, we are especially indebted to Mr. Wm. Payne, of Cleveland, for allowing us to make selections from his book entitled "Cleveland Illustrated," published by him in 1876.

The expenses of this book have been very great; the engraving, printing, paper, etc., being of the very best quality and latest style, and we hope it will meet with ready sale.

The compiler,

JOHN. S. REESE.

CANTON, O., September 1st, 1880.

SUMMIT COUNTY

AGRICULTURAL SOCIETY!

October 5, 6, 7 and 8, 1880.

THIRTY-FIRST MEETING.

————Fair to be held at————

FOUNTAIN PARK,

Five minutes drive from the business part of the city of Akron.

*Three Rail Roads passing through or near to and within one min-
ute's walk of our grounds, with half rates
on all the Roads.*

THE FINEST AND

MOST ROMANTIC GROUNDS IN THE STATE.

Water from stream, pond or lake; fountains in all parts of the grounds.

The Best County Fair in the State of Ohio.

20,000 people on the grounds in 1879, at one time.

The Best of Music, with two Bands each day. Horse
Trotting, with heavy purses. Chariot
Races each day.

EVERYBODY COME AND HAVE A GOOD TIME.

The Best Dining Hall in the State and the best women to attend to it. Come everybody
and have a good time, and look at the best stock in the country
and the best products of the country.

S. H. PITKIN, President,   H. A. PECK, Treasurer,
W. MILLER, Vice President,   J. H. CHRISTY, Secretary.

Brainard's Block, Cleveland.—(See page 57.)

CLEVELAND TO CANTON.

A Complete Description of the Scenery, objects of interest, etc., etc., along the line of the VALLEY RAILWAY.

KEEP THIS BEFORE YOU AS YOU RIDE ALONG.

"ALL ABOARD." We leave the Seneca street depot and ride for two miles through the old bed of the Ohio Canal, passing various manufactories, shops, &c., on either side. After riding two miles we arrive at the BROADWAY station, near the corner of Jefferson street ; on the right is the transfer track going up to the N. Y., P., & O. road which we have just passed under. Soon after leaving Broadway we cross the Cuyahoga River. After crossing the river, to the right is the turntable and engine house of the Valley Railway. The black building on the right a little further on, is the Valley Zinc Paint works, to the left in the distance can be seen the houses of the Cleveland Ice Companies. The city now begins to fade from our view, and our journey has fairly begun. We now ride four miles and half through the beautiful valley, now and then passing a bend in the river on our left, and occasionally we can see through to the left in the distance, buildings belonging to the Austin Powder Company. Four miles and a-half from Cleveland, we pass the powder switch which turns off to the warehouses of the powder company to the left. It is here where passengers get on and off for

BROOKLYN.

Over the hill to the right about a mile, is Brooklyn, a little further south is the village of Brighton. Two miles and a-half to the left is Newburg. About 300 feet south from this switch we can see the two brick charcoal houses of the powder company, on the opposite side of the canal to the left. Here charcoal is made to use in making powder. We next pass on the left, the extensive works of the Cleveland Dryer Company, which is very appropriately termed by the railroad men the "Stink Factory." The works are enclosed within a high board fence. Here the super-phosphates used by many farmers to fertilize their soil is manufactured. The bones and flesh of animals are prepared with sulphuric acid and reduced to a very fine powder, which is used to fertilize the soil. After passing this you can see the track ahead to the left as the road follows the bend of the river at this point, and the engine on a long train can be seen as it shoots around this graceful curve. We just get over this curve when the road makes a very long and quite sharp curve to the right, passing through the heart of the New York woods, which is just six miles from Cleveland. The name is derived from the fact that parties from New York purchased this tract several years ago with a view of speculation. The tallest trees along the line of the road are found in this woods. We come out of the woods and meet the river again and follow its winding course through the beautiful valley for four miles, passing through cool and shady groves, and then occasionally coming out upon the great open flats where almost as far as you can see is covered with flourishing farms, and in the distance the hills rise along the borders. You ride along with nothing to break the monotony of the scenery but the pleasing smiles of the train boy as he offers you pea nuts, fruits, and the like. If your teeth are bad and you can't chew pea nuts, ask for gum drops or taffy, these he always carries along for the old folks, and also for the young folks with false teeth.

Do you, as you ride through this wide and beautiful valley, realize the fact that at one period of the earth's history this was the bottom of a great river, and the tops of the hills on either side were its banks. This grand stream began with the world and has been gradually diminishing until it has almost dried up, being now a mere creek to what it was in primitive times. Fossil remains of animals and vegetation of gigantic proportions, but still resembling those of the present age, are constantly being unearthed in various localities. Thus we find everything diminishing as the world moves on, animal life, as well as water and plants. First, in the earths history we find an age of giants ; next—the present age—we find everything much smaller than that of the first, and it is the firm conviction of eminent scientists, that the next age will be an age of dwarfs, and life will continue to diminish in size with each succeeding age, and so on until it shall have entirely disappeared from the face of the earth. How long this will take, no one will attempt to state, but it will certainly come, as it has already been proven that the waters of the earth are fast drying up, and when the time comes, when there is no water on the earth, then life of all kind will cease ; then the earth will return to the heated condition as in the beginning, and time will be no more.

Three miles and a-half south of Brooklyn we pass the station of

WILLOW.

This was formerly called Eight Mile Lock on the canal, but recently a post office has been established near the acid works, and called Willow post office. There is no village here but only a small settlement back of the acid works. The long frame building you see to the left in the distance is the Acid Restoring Works. The process of restoring acid at these works is as follows : The Sulphuric acid after it has been used by the refineries at Cleveland for refining oil, is brought to the works in boats and is pumped out of the boats into separators, where the acid is separated from the tar by adding water ; the separated acid, as it is called, is then put into lead pans and then concentrated up to about 63 degrees, when it is put into glass retorts and concentrated up to 66 degrees which is commercial acid. It is then sent back to the refinery and used again. The tar that is taken out of the acid is used as fuel for concentrating the acid up to 63 degrees. The works below the acid works on the south side of the covered bridge is the Grindstone and Sickle Sharpener factory of A. C. Currier & Son, of Independence. One mile and a-half south, we pass another grindstone factory in the distance on the left. The grindstones made here are shipped by the canal which runs near it. The road now slides up close to the right side of the hill and runs this way for about half a-mile and then we arrive at

INDEPENDENCE.

The depot is on the left side of the track, the village is 1¼ miles to the right. After leaving here we travel for two miles along the west side of the valley and within sight of the river most of the way, with the broad open valley stretched out on our left with the Ohio canal along the opposite side of the valley. One mile south of Independence and 12 miles south of Cleveland, we pass

TINKER'S CREEK.

Tinker's creek, a small stream coming from the east, empties into the river at this point, and the 12 mile lock in the canal is about one-fourth mile to the left and there is a small settlement near it. At the iron bridge which crosses the river near the track, is where the passengers get on and off. The creek empties into the river about five hundred feet south, and the canal crosses the creek through an aqueduct. One mile further south we pass

BRECKSVILLE ROCK.

ALEXANDERS.

The 13-mile lock on the canal is just about half a mile to the left, and the large white grist mill of A. Alexander which can be seen from the cars after we come out on the open flat, is situated at this point ; this is the only grist mill in Independence township. There is no village here but only a few houses near the mill.

We travel on for another mile over the bottom lands of the valley and pass over Snake Flat No. 1. The hills begin to close in upon us and the road makes a long curve to the right, passing a deep cut through shale rock. The hills are now very near together, and we are riding through the Little Packsaddle Narrows. This is the most beautiful and striking spot along the line of the road and must be seen to be appreciated. Here we are between two great hills, almost mountains, with the Ohio canal along the opposite side and the Cuyahoga river flowing gently between us. This might be called the Eden of the Cuyahoga valley, for how much pleasanter a place would our first parents have wanted than this. We continue this way for about a mile when the hills separate and send us out over Snake Flat No. 2, at the tail of which is Brecksville station. If you will look back over the track we have just passed over, as the engine whistles for Brecksville, you will at once see by the shape in which the road crosses this flat, why we give it this name. We leave the flat and go around the great Brecksville Rock cut to the right. This cut is 50 feet high on the right and is composed of shale rock, (see illustration.) We now arrive at

BRECKSVILLE.

The depot is on the right and the village two miles to the right. As we leave the station, on our left can be seen the remains of a once flourishing saw mill, but it has not been used for several years and very little remains of it but the large chimney. We then cross Chippewa Creek and pass through the Great Hog Back, the deepest "cut" on the line; from the top of the hill to the bed of the track is 83 feet. It gets its name from the appearance of the hill before it was cut through and on account of the greasy nature of the clay of which the whole hill is composed. The long building on the left before entering the cut was used as a shelter for the laborers while engaged in grading the road at this point.

From Brecksville to Boston, a distance of four miles, we pass over the low lands of the valley with the great hills in the distance on each side of us, and the river twistingly twisting along to our left, when within about one mile of Boston we pass a frame one-story building to our right at the foot of the hill which is a cheese factory. A little further on we pass Joker's switch, here is where cross ties which are cut in the immediate neighborhood, are loaded on the cars and distributed along the road. Coming within about half a mile of Boston the river appears along side of us on the left, and we can see the saw mills, &c., of Boston on the opposite side of the river. The yellow building at the end of the dam is a saw mill,—we are now at

BOSTON.

The size and style of this city and Boston, Mass., are somewhat different, as you will certainly see before you leave. On the right is the depot and on our left is the Boston pic-nic grove, with dancing hall, refreshment stand, etc. After leaving this place we follow the river for about one mile. Only a short distance from Boston we round the Great Curve, (see engraving,) which is almost equal to the horse shoe curve of the Pennsylvania R. R. If you look ahead to the left you can see where the engine will soon be, which is almost beside you. Look down at the river on your left and then try to see the top of the rocks at your right. We next turn to our right and cross the river and Ohio canal by a trestle and bridge, (see engraving.) From the trestle, in the distance on the left can be seen the houses of the Lake Erie Ice Co. Ice is cut from the canal basin which is in front of the houses, packed during the winter, and in the spring shipped to Cleveland by canal. At the foot of the hill on the left and near the bridge is a small saw mill. After crossing the bridge we pass through the "Devil's Passage," here we travel 1,000 feet entirely shut out from the world with nothing to see

BURROWS BROTHERS,

324 & 328 Euclid Avenue,

CLEVELAND, O.

——AND——

STATIONERY.

ALBUMS,   BIBLES,

ENGRAVINGS,   GAMES,

WEDDING GIFTS,

SCHOOL SUPPLIES, INKS,

BLANK BOOKS, POCKET BOOKS.

WHOLESALE & RETAIL.

but the ragged rocks on each side which almost touch the cars. The engine whistles for Peninsula while we are in the passage. On the side of the hill to the right before we arrive at the depot can be seen the long clay slides of a brick yard. We now stop at

PENINSULA.

On the left is the depot and on the right the Peninsula Mills and the dam which had to be made when the course of the river was changed by the railway. To the right of the mill the canal crosses the river by an aqueduct : (see the diagram of the river at this point in connection with the history of Peninsula in another part of the book.) As we leave Peninsula we pass various saw mills, planing mills, &c., with the river on our right. One half a mile south of Peninsula we cross the river and canal. To the right from the bridge, the Penisula stone quarries are located. We now begin to leave the low valley and begin slowly to ascend to the top of the hill, and continue along for three miles on the west side of the valley with the canal most of the time near us on the left and the river winding along down in the valley. One and a-half miles from Peninsula we pass a boat yard on the left, and a little further on we pass a steam saw mill. The great open piece of bottom land in the valley to the left about one mile from Peninsula, was tilled by the Indians many centuries before the whites came here. It was under cultivation when this country was first visited by the whites, and although it stood in the midst of a dense forest there was not the slightest evidence of a stump or root upon it, showing that it must have been many years since the trees were cut from it. In cultivating it now great quantities of stone arrow heads, axes and knives are found. We have now traveled three miles and arrive at

EVERETT.

The depot is on the right side of the track. One mile south of this place we pass through the gravel cut, here large quantites of gravel is procured for ballasting the road. Just before we pass through this cut the road brings us across the clearing where the Indians, in the early days of the country's history, held their feasts and jollifications, the Indians for hundreds of miles around came here at certain times to join in the frolics. Just over the gravel bank to the left are the remains of an ancient fortification which are well constructed and are probably the work of the mound builders, and must date back long before the Indians. A tree growing on it was cut some time since, and by counting the rings upon it denoting its age, it proved to be 250 years old, so that the fortification was erected long before that time. This Cuyahoga valley must have been a favorite retreat for the various tribes of Indians. One mile and a-half from Everett we pass

HAWKINS.

There is nothing here but a cheese factory, on the left side of the track. The bridge over the canal at the cheese factory has for many years been called "Hawkins Bridge," and the station has been called from that. There is no village within several miles of the station. One mile from Hawkins we pass an old saw mill on our left. One and a-half miles south of Hawkins we arrive at

BOTZUMS.

The 'cut' we pass through just before arriving at the station was an Indian burying ground, the top of this hill is flat and level. During the construction of the road several skeletons and implements were unearthed in this 'cut.' On the right is the depot and on the left is the large warehouse, which was used in the early days of the canal. About five hundred feet south of the depot we pass between two ancient Indian mounds. The one on our left is at the rear of a house that faces the canal. This is a small round

mound with a tree at the top. The mound on our right is large and more square shaped, with a flat, table-like top. After continuing for two and a-half miles along the west bank of the canal, passing through several cool and shady groves and beautiful open flats, we pass

OLD PORTAGE.

This name is derived from the fact that "The Portage Path" started from the Cuyahoga river at a point directly east of the white bridge, which crosses the canal on our left and continued south-west to New Portage on the Tuscarawas River, a distance of about twelve miles. The path crossed the railroad about where the present road crossing is. The Indians came up the Cuyahoga in their canoes to Old Portage and then carried them over the portage path to the Tuscarawas at New Portage. There is no village near this station now, but it is a getting on and off place for the surrounding country.—(See history of Old Portage). One mile and a half from Portage we enter the Big Narrows— (see engraving), and begin to ascend at the rate of 40 feet to the mile, and continue to ascend at this rate till we reach a point four miles south of East Akron. Here we pass through cut after cut, varying in height from 40 to 80 feet ; the first cut and the one which is shown in the engraving is 80 feet high. If you notice when you pass Portage, that the canal is but a few feet below us, but when we get to Akron we cross it on a trestle 32 feet above the water, after we have passed about five locks in the canal which average each 10 feet high, thus making us about 95 feet higher at Akron than we were two and a-half miles north. As we enter the Narrows we see the last of the Cuyahoga River, which we have followed ever since we left Cleveland. At a point near the covered bridge, which can be seen in the distance to the left, as we enter the Narrows, the river takes a direct turn eastward. Here its branch, called the Little Cuyahoga, empties into it, which we now see down in the valley as we continue on. When we are about one mile from the Akron depot, we can see a part of Akron by looking ahead to the left ; the depot can also be seen on the side of the hill. The grain\elevator of F. Schumacher, and Buchtel College are the highest buildings and can be seen above the others. Before we arrive at the depot we cross the Cascade Trestle, which is 500 feet long and 32 feet above the water, and then cross the bridge over Howard Street. To the right from the trestle is the Aetna Mills, and to our left the Cascade Mills. As we cross Howard Street, we see to the left the Great Chuckery Cut, or what is generally called Sand Hill. It was excavated about eight years ago to make a short road to Cuyahoga Falls. In the valley close to our left is the Akron Gas Works, and on the right, the depot and freight house.

The train stops, and we are at the city of

AKRON.

We leave the depot and pass around the north-east part of the city to the East Akron depot, a distance of two and one-half miles. A short distance from the Akron depot, we pass by the remains of the old Akron Oil Refinery which was destroyed by fire several years ago; nothing now remains but a few old buildings and a tank or two. One mile from the depot we pass through the Summit County Fair Grounds, and over the Great Trestle, (see engraving) which is 1,000 feet long and 44 feet high. The Little Cuyahoga makes a curve here, thus the trestle has to cross it twice. The large brick building seen to the right from the trestle will be used as a sewer pipe works by parties in East Akron. Beyond this, and a little higher up, the N. Y. P. & O., and the C. Mt. V. & C. Railroads, which have been running side by side from New Portage, five miles west of Akron, divide here and branch off in different directions. The settlement here is called Old Forge, from the fact of a steam forge having been started here, and afterwards removed to Akron ; but a few years ago it was moved back to its former location. The Akron Steam Forge is to the right as you pass between the two railroads. The transfer track from the

CITY HOTEL,

CLEVELAND, O.

The most centrally located hotel in the city, being on Seneca Street, next to the new Court House, and but one half block from Superior Street.

Fare and beds as good as any hotel in the city, and the price is but **1.50 per day.** Commercial men will find good accommodations and an old friend,

H. B. WEST,

Founder of the Put in Bay House and formerly of the West House, Sandusky, O.

BAYRD & GOLDSTEIN,

88 Seneca St., Cleveland, O.,

Manufacturers, offer at wholesale and retail, the largest stock and best variety to be found in the State, at prices as low as New York, Boston or Chicago, comprising

MOULDINGS, FRAMES, CHROMOS,

Cornices, Velvet Frames, Easels,

Reward Cards, Scrap Book Pictures, &c., &c.

Persons visiting the city are cordially invited to call and examine.

☞ FRAMES OF ALL KINDS MADE TO ORDER. ☜

3

VALLEY RAILWAY up to the C. Mt. V. & C. R. R., is also on the right. On the left is the great gravel bank of the road. Most of the gravel used for ballasting the road is taken from here. From here to the East Akron depot, the old Pennsylvania and Ohio canal is to our right, with the little track of the Sewer Pipe Works of East Akron running along the tow-path. The sewer pipe is carried from East Akron in small cars drawn by horses, and loaded on the cars of the other roads at Old Forge.

As the engine whistles for East Akron, we cross the Little Cuyahoga and the old canal, and pass along the various sewer pipe and stone ware works. The first one to the left after crossing the canal, is the Akron Stone Ware Company's, whose adv. appears in

GREAT CURVE NEAR BOSTON.

this work. Coming to the depot, we cross the little river again. It is here dammed for water power. To the right in the distance is the new Second M. E. Church of Akron. We now arrive at the depot of

EAST AKRON.

The depot is on the right of the track, back of which is the Fine Ware Works. We leave the depot and pass under East Market Street through a tunnel—but boys kiss your girls quick, for it is a short one, and you will be "caught in the act." We cross the river for the last time, and pass several stone ware works to our right. About five hundred feet from the depot we pass through an old pottery, which was in the way of the road and had to be cut through, thus part is on each side of the track. We next pass the Akron Straw Board Works along to our left.

We now leave the valley and enter the coal regions of Ohio, and travel over the fertile rolling lands of the interior. Three-fourths of a mile south of East Akron we pass through a cool and shady grove, and as we come out on a small opening, a stone ware shop can be seen down in the valley at our left. Next we pass **Coal Switch,** which runs off from our right to the bank of the Middlebury Coal Company, one and a half miles distant. The shaft of this bank can be seen to the right, when we get two miles farther south. Before the VALLEY RAILWAY was constructed through here,

coal was brought from this bank to East Akron over a three foot track ; traces of this little road can be seen near the VALLEY RAILWAY to the right, as we pass through East Akron, south of the depot.

Two miles south of East Akron, after we have passed under the over-head bridge, the forty-foot grade ends, which we have been coming up for the last six miles. Three miles from East Akron we can see one of the Springfield Potteries in the distance on our left. On our right in the distance can be seen the shaft of the coal bank and the long dwelling houses of the miners.

About the time the engine whistles for Krumroy, we pass the switch which runs off on the right to a coal bank three and a-half miles distant.

Four miles south of East Akron we arrive at

KRUMROY.

The depot is on the left, but there is no village within several miles of the station (see history of Springfield). All the streams that appear up to this station feed the Cuyahoga River. The waters that appear between here and Greentown feed the Tuscarawas River. The surface is of a rolling nature from here to Canton, and is a very rich grain producing country, wheat and corn being raised in abundance. Three miles south of Krumroy we pass through the Millheim mill pond ; the large mill can be seen in the distance to the left, a short distance before we pass the pond.

Four miles from Krumroy we arrive at

UNIONTOWN.

As we come to the station, on our right we pass a grain warehouse. Grain is brought here from the surrounding country and shipped on the cars to Akron. The depot is on the left, and the settlement on the right is called Myersville. It was settled since the VALLEY ROAD has been built. Uniontown village is one mile to the left of the station. A hack runs regular from the station to the village. The engine generally takes water here when going south, and going north they take water at Peninsula. As we leave the station we pass a saw mill on our right, and one mile and a half south of Uniontown, we strike the Greentown Plain. Here for two miles the track runs in a straight line. About the middle of this plain, we pass through a vast huckleberry swamp. At the end of this plain the engine whistles for Greentown station, and we pass around a curve to the right. As we round this curve we pass the beautiful little grove to our left, owned by Mr. J. A. Borst, of Greentown(see engraving). At this point we pass over the great water-shed of the State, which extends from the east, westward across the State. Here in this grove the water can be seen to divide, part going to Lake Erie and part to the Ohio River. The elevation at this point is about 555 feet above Lake Erie. All the streams that appear between here and Canton, are feeders to the Nimishillen. A little farther on and we arrive at

GREENTOWN.

The depot is on the right. The village of Greentown is about three-fourths of a mile to the left, and the village of Greensburg is two and a half miles to the right ; both places use this depot. The old log hut on the side of the hill to the right soon after leaving the depot, is the birth-place of Lewis Miller, Esq., now of Akron, and one of the proprietors of the Buckeye Mower and Reaper Works. Look upon this humble cottage, his birthplace

and then at his elegant mansion in Akron, and see what patience and labor has done. A little further south on the left is the coal bank of Smith, Borst & Company. (see adv.) A side track runs from the VALLEY ROAD to the bank. A little farther on, to the left, is the Drain Tile Works of Isaac Stripe, and the shop back of this is the Sewer Pipe Works of H. & I. Stripe.—(see advs.)

One mile south of Greentown we strike the Berlin Plain, which is two and a half miles without a curve, and is the longest straight piece of track along the line. We pass through a pleasant grove and come out upon the open plain on a long curve to the left, while on the curve the remains of an old saw mill can be seen to the left. A little farther on, the long white building is the meeting house of the curious sect of people called "Dunkards." They hold meetings here twice a month, on Sunday, and members for twenty-five miles around come here to join in. Still farther on, to the left, we see a brick school-house, beside which is a country meeting house called Zion's Church. Almost directly in front of this is Kropf's red Brewery, which can be plainly seen from the cars. We next arrive at

NEW BERLIN.

The station is on the left of the track, on the side of which is the Portable Saw-mill of Joseph Marchand. The station is in Jackson Township, Stark County, but the village of New Berlin is in Plain Township, one mile to the left of the depot.

From here to Red Mill, a distance of three miles, the road passes through the woods, occasionally coming out upon an open space among the hills, where flourishing farms can be seen in all directions. Two miles south of New Berlin, the road passes around to the right of a small mountain, termed Meadow Grove Peak. One side, and the top is covered with tall trees and underbrush, while the side to the track is a nice green meadow. One mile further on we pass the

RED MILL.

The mill to the left used to be red, but has not been used for over six years, and the paint has almost deserted it. The saw mill at the side of it is running most of the time. The mill will also start up again soon. There is no village or settlement within several miles of the mill. One half a mile south of the Red Mill to the right, the West Branch of the Nimishillen Creek appears, which consists mostly of swamp from here to Canton, caused by damming in various places to make water-power for the mills. If you look ahead to the right, as we come around the curve soon after passing Red Mill, you can see down the creek for over two miles, which is a very striking view. One mile south of Red Mill we pass a coal bank with a side track running to it on the left. One half a mile farther south we pass the White Mill on our left. About three hundred feet south of the mill is the crossing called

LAKE PARK.

Here passengers get off for Lake Park, at Myer's Lake which is one mile to the right. A large hotel is on the grounds, and every convenience for pleasure seekers. On the left at the crossing is where an attempt to procure coal was made some years ago, but proved a failure. The dam below the crossing is where the city of Canton receives its water supply. It is drawn from the dam on the opposite side, and carried along through a race to the water works which is one mile farther south, and then pumped through pipe

distributed over the city. Along that side of the hill are several places where attempts to open coal banks have been made, but with very small success. As the engine whistles for Canton, we can see the brewery on our right, and a little further on we pass the Canton Water Works, which is the building of brick with a tall smoke stack. The city of Canton now begins to appear on our left, and we arrive at

TUSCARAWAS AVENUE.

We continue on for another mile with the city along to our left, and the bed of the great Union Mill dam to our right. This dam was considered an unhealthy addition to the city, and was drawn off under the order of the City Council about one year ago. Before arriving at the depot we pass the turn-table and engine-house to our right.—the train stops, and we are at the crossing of the P. F. W. & C. R. R. On our left is the depot and the city of

CANTON.

This is the end of the road, and all passengers get off here. Many feeling glad to get home, but sorry to leave such a beautiful panorama of natural scenery which is furnished by no other road than the VALLEY RAILWAY.

The "OLD MOUNTAINEER."

DR. GEORGE FERRARD,

Now in his 88th. year, better known as the "Old Mountaineer," the oldest practicing Physician in Ohio,

Cures Cancer without useing Knife or Plasters

Effectually killing the Cancer in 15 minutes with but little pain. Effectually removing it Root and Branch in 8 days, and healing it as easily as any ordinary sore.

Cures Ulcers of all kinds, Gravel, Diabetes, all Urinary Troubles, Liver, Kidneys, Heart, Bronchitis, Tetter, Scrofula, Scald Head

And all Cutaneous Eruptions. Two years in Akron, where he is permanently located in **Howard Street, over Spangler's Hat Store.**

ADDRESS, OLD MOUNTAINEER, AKRON, OHIO.

Enclosing stamp for return answer. Medicines sent by Express to any place in the United States C. O. D. Treats any and all Old Chronic Disease. Female Complaints a specialty.

4

CANTON TO CLEVELAND.

A brief Description of the Scenery, and Objects of Interest along the line.

KEEP THIS BEFORE YOU AS YOU RIDE ALONG.

"ALL ABOARD" for Cleveland and intermediate points. We now take our seats and are ready to take in the scenery of the VALLEY RAILWAY. We will not attempt to re-describe the scenery which has already been described in the trip from Cleveland here, but only mention the prominent points and refer you to the preceding pages for a full and complete description of the sights along the road. The history of each station appears further on in the work.

Passing from the depot to **Tuscarawas Avenue**, a distance of one mile, we have the city of Canton on our right, and the old bed of the Union Dam to our left.—(See page 24) Soon after leaving Tuscarawas Avenue station, we pass the Canton Water Works and a Brewery on our left, and have the West Branch of the Nimishillen Creek on our left, from here to the Red Mill.

All the streams that appear between Canton and Greentown flow into the Nimishil-len. Two miles and a-half north of Canton, we pass **Lake Park,** formerly called White Mill. The mill is on the right at this point. Myer's Lake is one mile to the left, and is a very beautiful place, with a hotel on the grounds and every convenience for visitors. One-half mile north of Lake Park we pass a coal bank with a switch running up to it on our right. One and a-half miles north of Lake Park, we pass **Red Mill** on our right, (see page 22). One mile north of Red Mill we pass Meadow-Grove Peak on our left. This is a large hill resembling a mountain, and has a grove on the top and one side, and a beautiful sloping meadow on the side toward the track. Three miles from Red Mill, we arrive at **New Berlin.** The depot is on the right. A portable saw-mill is at the side of it. The village is one mile to the right. We are now on the Berlin Plain, which is two and a-half miles long, and is the longest straight piece of track on the road, (see page 22). A little south of New Berlin, to our right we pass Kropf's Brewery, and behind this is the country meeting house called Zion's Church, beside this is the District School Building. A little further on the long white building is the "Dunkards" meeting house, (see page 22). We now leave the Plain on a curve to the right, and as we round this curve, the remains of an old saw mill can be seen to our right. As the engine whistles for Greentown we pass the Drain Tile Works of Isaac Stripe, back of which is the Sewer Pipe Works of H. & I. Stripe. On the right still further on, we pass the coal bank of Smith, Borst & Company. A side track runs off to it on the right. These firms are represented in this book in connection with the history of Greentown. The log hut

on the side of the hill to the left before we arrive at the station is the birth-place of Lewis Miller, Esq., now of the Buckeye Works at Akron.

We now arrive at **Greentown.** The depot is on the left, and the village is three-fourths of a mile to the right, and Greensburg is two and a-half miles to the left. About five hundred feet north of the depot we cross the great water-shed of the State, (see page 20). In the beautiful grove to the right, (see engraving) the water can be seen to divide, part going to the Ohio River and part to Lake Erie. The elevation here is about 555 feet above Lake Erie. We now pass over the Greentown Plain, which is two miles of straight track over the bottom lands and marshes. The streams that appear between here and Krumroy feed the Tuscarawas River. Three and a-half miles north of Greentown we arrive at **Uniontown.** As we come to the depot, we pass a saw-mill on the left. Great

TRESTLE AND BRIDGE NEAR PENINSULA, (See page 12.)

numbers of ties for the road have been sawed here. The village is one mile to the right. The small settlement on the left of the depot is called Myersville, which has been settled since the railroad has been built. As we leave the depot we pass a grain warehouse on our left. Grain from the surrounding country is brought here and shipped over the VALLEY ROAD to the Akron mills. One mile north of Uniontown, we pass through the Millheim mill pond, the mill being situated some distance to the right and can be seen in the distance when we get a little further on.

Four miles north of Uniontown, we arrive at **Krumroy,** formerly called Springfield. There is no village near the station. A short distance north of the depot we pass a switch on our left, which runs back to a coal bank 3½ miles distant. One mile north of Krumroy, we can see in the distance to the left, the shaft of a coal bank and the long dwelling houses of the miners. A little further on to our right, one of the Springfield

Potteries can be seen in the distance. Two miles from Krumroy, we strike the Forty-foot Grade as we pass under the over-head bridge. We now travel for six miles down hill at the rate of forty feet to the mile. A little further on to the left we pass **Coal Switch,** which runs out one and a-half miles to the coal bank which you passed to the left a few minutes ago. To our right, as we come out upon an opening soon after passing the switch, we see a stone ware works in the valley below. As we pass through the cool and shady grove, the engine whistles for East Akron. As we pass along, on our left can be seen the traces of the little coal road from the coal bank which we have just passed. Coal was brought here over this three foot track before the VALLEY RAILWAY was built, but since the switch has been put in from the VALLEY RAILWAY, the little track has been torn up. On our right we pass the Akron Straw Board Works, and on our left we pass several stone-ware works, and then cross the Little Cuyahoga River. Before arriving at the depot we pass under East Market Street, through the only tunnel on the road, and arrive at **East Akron.** The depot is on the left, back of which is the Fine Ware Works. We leave the depot, cross the river again, and pass several sewer pipe-works on each side. To the left, while crossing the river, is the Second M. E. Church of Akron. Soon after leaving the depot we cross the old Pennsylvania and Ohio Canal and Little Cuyahoga River. We next pass under the N. Y. P. & O. R. R., and about six hundred feet further we pass under the C. Mt. V. & C. R. R. The settlement here is called Old Forge. Between the two roads on our right is the great gravel bank of the road. Most of the gravel used in ballasting the road has been taken from here. On our left is the Akron Steam Forge and the transfer track running from the VALLEY RAILWAY up to the C. Mt. V. & C. R. R. Along the old Pennsylvania and Ohio Canal is the small track running from the Sewer Pipe Works at East Akron to this place. Sewer pipe is carried from there in cars drawn by horses, and loaded on the C. Mt. V. & C. R. R. cars at this point. The settlement here is called Old Forge. We now slack up and cross the great trestle, (see frontispiece engraving), over the Akron Fair Grounds and the Little Cuyahoga River twice. The mills of the Austin Powder Company, now at Five Mile Lock near Cleveland, was at one time situated in this valley below. They blew up about fifteen years ago, and then removed to their present location. This trestle is 1,000 feet long and 44 feet high. The large brick building seen to the left is to be used as a sewer pipe works by parties from East Akron. Back of this and a little higher up, the N. Y. P. & O., and the C. Mt. V. & C. R. R., which have been running side by side for about ten miles separate, each going in different directions. · As the engine whistles for Akron we pass through where once stood the Akron Oil Refinery, which was destroyed by fire some years ago. Nothing but a few old buildings and a tank on each side of the track marks the spot.

We now arrive at **Akron.** The depot is on our left, and the city also. The Akron Gas Works is to our right in the valley. As we leave the depot, we cross over Howard Street ; to the right is the great "Chuckery Cut," or what is usually called Sand Hill. This was opened about eight years ago to make a short road to Cuyahoga Falls. We then cross the Cascade Trestle, which is over the Ohio Canal ; it is 500 feet long and 32 feet above the water. On the right are the Cascade Mills, and on the left are the Aetna Mills.

We now travel for two and a-half miles through the Big Narrows, passing through one cut after another, varying in height from 40 to 80 feet. The last one is 80 feet high, (see engraving). At this point ends the 40 foot grade, but the grade is still very steep until we reach Peninsula. In the distance to the right, as we come out of the Narrows, is the covered bridge, where the Big Cuyahoga River coming from the east, is met by the the Little River, both uniting and making one stream, which appears all the way from here to Cleveland.

Four miles north of Akron we pass **Old Portage,** (see page 16).

Two miles and a-half north of Portage, we arrive at **Botzums.** Just before we arrive at the depot, which is to our left, we pass between two beautiful Indian mounds ; a small round one to our right, with a tall tree on its very summit. The one to the left is large and square-shaped and about fifteen feet high. As we leave Botzums, we pass through a 'cut,' the top of which is very flat and level, and was once the burying ground of the Indians of this section. In the construction of the road at this point, several skeletons were unearthed, together with many implements. One-half a mile north of Botzums, we pass a saw mill on our right. One mile and a-half north of Botzums, we pass **Hawkins.** To the right is a cheese factory. The bridge over the canal near the factory has for many years been known as "Hawkin's Bridge," and the station has been named from that. One-half a mile north is the "gravel cut"; great quantities of gravel are taken from here and used for ballasting the road. Just over this bank to the right, are the remains of an ancient fortification, which are well constructed and are probably the work of the Mound Builders, and must date back long before the Indians. A tree growing upon it was cut some time ago, and by counting the rings upon it denoting its age, it was found to be two hundred and fifty years old, so that the fortification was erected long before that time. After passing through this cut we cross an open clearing, which was the place where the Indians of this section held their feasts and jollifications during the early days of the country's history. This Cuyahoga Valley must have been a favorite retreat for the Indians, as the remains of them can be found all through the valley.

One mile from here we arrive at **Everett.** The depot is on the left and the village on the right. One and a-half miles north of Everett, we pass a steam saw mill to our right, and a little further on we pass a boat yard on the same side. The great open piece of land in the valley to our right a little further north, is called "Indian Farm." It was tilled by the Indians many centuries before the whites came here. It was under cultivation when this country was first visited by the whites, and although it stood in the midst of a dense forest, there was not the slightest evidence of a stump or root upon it, showing that it must have been many years since the trees were cut from it. In cultivating it now great quantities of stone arrow-heads, axes and knives are found. We now cross the Ohio Canal and Cuyahoga River. To the left are the Peninsula Stone Quarries. We now pass along saw mills, planing mills, &c., with the river and canal on our left. We pass through the village and arrive at the **Peninsula** depot. To the right is the depot, and to the left are the Peninsula mills and the dam in the river ; the course of the river has been changed by the Railroad here, thus necessitating the construction of a dam.—(See diagram of river with the history of Peninsula in this book). On the north side of the mill, the canal crosses the river through an aqueduct. We now leave Peninsula and pass through the Devil's Passage, (see page 12), and over the canal and river and then around the Great Bend, (see engravings). From the trestle you can see the houses of the Lake Erie Ice Company in the distance to the right. When the engine whistles for Boston, you can see to the right on the opposite side of the river, the clay mills of an old brick-yard. We now arrive at **Boston.**

The depot is on the left and the village on the right. To the right of the depot are pic-nic grounds. After leaving the depot and passing the covered bridge over the river to our right, we can see the village, with several saw mills, &c. The yellow building at the opposite end of the dam is a saw mill. About one mile north of Boston, we pass Joker's Switch on the left. Here cross ties, which are cut in the neighboring woods, are loaded on the cars and distributed along the road. A little further on to the left we pass a cheese factory. Three miles further on we pass through the Great Hog Back, which is the deepest 'cut' on the road, being 83 feet from the top to the bed of the track. It derives its name from the appearance of the hill before it was cut through, and from the fact that the clay of which it is composed, is of a greasy nature. We pass through it, cross Chippewa Creek and arrive at **Brecksville** station. On the right side of the hill as

THE NEW BUCKEYE MOWER, WITH TABLE RAKE.

Will Cut any kind of Grain, and in any Condition it may be found, doing thoroughly Clean Work, and without waste deliver the gavel in the best possible shape for the binders.

Manufactured by AULTMAN, MILLER & CO., Akron, Ohio.

we come out, is the shanty where the laborers stayed while excavating this 'cut.' On the opposite side of the river are the remains of an old saw mill ; very little more than the tall chimney now remains. The Brecksville depot is on the left and the village is two miles from the depot to the left.

We leave the depot and pass around the Brecksville Rock (see engraving) on a curve to the left. This cut is 50 feet high on the left and is composed of shale rock. We now come out on **Snake Flat No. 2**, then pass along through the Little Packsaddle Narrows, then over Snake Flat No. 1.—(For a full description of this beautiful spot see page 12).. We then pass **Alexanders**, (see page 11), and one mile north we pass Tinker's Creek, (see page 11). The canal here crosses Tinker's Creek through an aqueduct, and can be seen to the right a little south of the iron bridge over the river.

One and one-third miles further on we arrive at **Independence.** The depot is on the right, and the village is one and one-fourth miles to the left. One mile north of here, we pass a Grind Stone Works on the right in the distance. Grindstones of all sizes are made here and shipped mostly over the canal, which runs along the side of the works. Two miles and a-half from Independence, we pass **Willow**, (see page 10). The Acid Restoring Works, which is the long building to the right of the track, is the only object to mark this point, (see page 10). Two miles north of Willow, we pass through the New York Woods, (see page 9), on a long curve to the left. The tallest trees along the line of the road are found in this woods. We are now just six miles from Cleveland. We come out of the woods and pass the works of the Cleveland Dryer Company on the right, (see page 9). You will smell this place before you see it. The railroad men call it the "Stink Factory," and you will agree with them before you get past it. A little further north, to the right can be seen the two brick buildings which are the charcoal houses of the Austin Powder Company which is located all through the valley above. We now pass the Powder Switch which runs in on the right to the warehouses of the Powder Company. Here at the crossing is where the passengers for BROOKLYN get on and off.

Brooklyn is situated about one mile to the left, and a little farther south is the village of Brighton. Newburg is two and a-half miles to the right.

For the next two miles as we go along, we can occasionally see some of the buildings of the Powder Company in the distance to the right. Two miles from Brooklyn as we are passing through the woods, the engine whistles for Cleveland. As we come out of the woods the black building to our left is the Zinc Paint Works, and in the distance to the right can be seen the houses of the Cleveland Ice Companies. The train comes to a stop before it crosses the Cuyahoga River Bridge, and then proceeds carefully. To the left as we cross the bridge is the turn-table and engine-house of the VALLEY RAIL-WAY. We now arrive at the Broadway station, which is near the corner of Jefferson Street. To the left is the transfer track running to the N. Y. P. & O. Railroad, which we will soon pass under.

We leave Broadway and travel two miles through the bed of the old Ohio Canal, passing shops and manufactories of various kinds on either side of us. The train stops— the brakeman yells out "Cleveland," and we all get off. To the right is the depot at the foot of Seneca Street. Five minutes walk will stand you on Superior Street. How much nearer would you want a railroad to bring you ? When you take your ride back, take this book and follow the description as you go along. We have now described the scenery and points of interest along the line and in the following pages we will give you as complete a history as could be had of each station on the road, illustrating all the prominent points of interest in each place.

HISTORICAL SKETCHES.

Of the Various Stations Along the Line of the Valley Railway.

CITY OF CLEVELAND.

CLEVELAND was originally spelled "Cleaveland," after General Moses Cleaveland, of the State of Connecticut, who, in company with other members of a surveying party sent out out by the Connecticut Land Company to survey their recently purchased property on the "Connecticut Western Reserve," entered the mouth of the Cuyahoga, from the Lake, on the 22d. of July, 1796. General Cleaveland left men at the river to put up buildings for the surveyors, and proceeded with the remainder of the party to Sandusky. A few cabins and a store house were erected, and on the return of the remainder of the party, later in the season, the work of laying out a town was performed under the superintendence of Augustus Porter. They surveyed a tract about one mile square for the town. He made a plot of this piece, laying it off into streets and lots. Mr. Porter surveyed most of the streets himself, and then left the work in charge of Mr. Holley to complete the survey of lots. The survey of the city was commenced on the 16th. of September, and completed about the 1st. of October, 1796. The party returned to Connecticut on the 18th. of October, leaving but three persons behind, Job Stiles and wife, and Joseph Landon, with provisions for the winter. Landon soon abandoned the spot, and his place was taken by Edward Paine, who came from the State of New York, for the purpose of trading with the Indians, and who may be considered the first mercantile man who transacted business in Cleveland. Thus during the winter of 1796-7, the population of the city consisted of three inhabitants. In the ensuing year, 1797, several additions were made to the population of the new settlement—several families arrived and a Mr. Chapman brought with him two yoke of oxen and four cows. The first wedding took place in this year between Miss Chloe Inches and Mr. William Clement, of Erie, who had arrived here soon after Miss Inches. The marriage ceremony was performed by Mr. Seth Hart, of the surveying party, who had acted as their chaplain. During the next three years considerable progress was made by the new settlement. The population which at the beginning of 1798 numbered fifteen, was increased in 1799 by the arrival of two families, one of which numbered nine persons. These two families were ninety-two days on their way from Connecticut. In 1800 several other families came, and other houses were put up in different parts of the plateau, upon which the city east of the river now stands. A township school was organized in this year and taught by a Sarah Doane. The first sermon was preached in this year by Rev. Joseph Badger, who was sent out by the Connecticut Missionary Society.

When the settlement was five years old, in 1801, the "first families" of Cleveland, determined to celebrate the "Glorious Fourth" by a grand ball. As it

CLEVELAND IN 1800.

proved one of the greatest successes of the time, we publish a complete account of it, which may be interesting to many, especially those who attend dances at the present day, and know how it is themselves. "The *elite* of Cleveland were there. As every white person in the settlement belonged to the *elite*, it followed that all who were able to dance, or drink new whiskey, or see others do so, were promptly on hand at the appointed time. Thirty persons took part in the ceremonies of the occasion. Major Samuel Jones presided at the fiddle and called off the figures. John Wood, Benjamin Wood and R. H. Blinn were the floor managers. How one couple went to the ball has been put on record by the beau of the occasion. Distiller Bryant's son Gilman, was among the invited guests. Gilman Bryant was then seventeen years old, and had taken a fancy to a Miss Doane, who had recently arrived at the Corners. The young lady, fourteen years old, was solicited to accompany Gilman Bryant to the ball, and graciously consented. Gilman dressed himself in a fashionable suit of the period, made up of gingham, *queued* his hair with a yard and a-half of black ribbon to the size and thickness of a corncob, greased it with a candle and plastered it with flour, tied on his heavy brogans and donned his wool hat, mounted his "Dobbin gray," like the wooer in the old ballad, and jogged off to the cabin of the Doans. Miss Doan was anxiously awaiting his coming, and lost no time in fixing her toilet. Mounting a stump by the side of the cabin, she spread her under petticoat on the old horse behind her beau, rolled up her calico dress to keep it clean, jumped up and putting her arm around her companion's waist, rode off in a state of enjoyment. They found the company assembled at Major Carter's house, ready to begin. Major Jones' fiddle gave a preliminary squeak, the couples took their places, and then away they went to the tune of "Fisher's Hornpipe" or "Hi Betty Martin." How the heavy brogans drummed away on the rough puncheon floor in the scamper-down, double-shuffle, western-swing and half-moon ! When the dancers grew heated, or the fiddler's elbow needed greasing, Bryant's whiskey, sweetened with maple sugar, refreshed the former and limbered the latter. It is doubtful if any dance, since Cleveland has reached the dignity of the second city of Ohio, afforded more unalloyed enjoyment, than that Fourth of July ball in Major Carter's log-cabin seventy-five years ago."

In 1815 Cleveland assumed importance as a village, the Legislature of the preceding year having granted it a charter. The year following, the first bank in the village was opened, under the name of "The Commercial Bank of Lake Erie," with Leonard Case as president. The year succeeding, 1817, was memorable for the organization of the first religious body in the settlement. Before this the inhabitants of Cleveland had regarded christianity with scorn, and religion had become a theme for coarse jesting and ridicule. A distillery was built soon after the first settlement, and all, even the "first families," became its regular and profitable customers. The religious element gradually found place, and in 1817 an organization of the Episcopal Church was formed, with Rev. Roger Searles as pastor. Meetings were held wherever a room could be procured until, in 1828, the corporation of Trinity Church was formed, and a frame building was erected on the corner of St. Clair and Seneca Streets, which for the next quarter of a century became well known as "Old Trinity." The first newspaper published in the place was the Cleveland *Gazette and Commercial Register*, which appeared on the 31st. of July, 1818, and was issued weekly for a while and then at different intervals, till it soon passed out of existence to give way to the *Herald*, which began publication the following year. On the 1st. of September, 1818, the first steamer ever seen on Lake Erie—the "Walk-in-the-water"—arrived in port. She was bound from Buffalo to Detroit, and her arrival and departure was greeted by several rounds of artillery.

In the year 1820, Cleveland began to connect itself with the outside world. In that year a coach began running between Cleveland and Columbus, and a few months later one was put on the line to Norwalk. Soon after coaches were started for Pittsburgh and Buffalo. In 1827 the Ohio Canal was opened between Akron and Cleveland, and among

PUBLIC SQUARE, NORTH-WEST SECTION, 1839.

the earliest shipments to Cleveland by canal, was that of the first load of coal. It was some time before the people could be induced to use the coal. They objected to its dirty, nasty appearance, and the offensive smoke, and placed little faith in the excellent qualities claimed for it. Cleveland now began to grow rapidly. In the year 1835, the rush of emigrants from the Eastern States to the west was immense. It received its charter as a city in 1836. About this time the fierce rivalry began between the settlements on the opposite sides of the Cuyahoga. In 1819 a Mr. Josiah Barber built a log-cabin on the west side of the river, and thus became the first permanent settler on that side. In 1031 the Buffalo Company purchased a tract on the west side, covering the low land towards the mouth of the river and the bluffs overlooking it. The low ground they studded with warehouses, and the bluffs with stores, residences and several fine hotels, and preparations were made for building a city that should eclipse the rival settlement east of the river. A short ship canal was made from the Cuyahoga to the old river bed at the east end, and the water being high, a steamer passed through a natural channel at the west end. When steps were taken to get a charter for Cleveland, negotiations were entered into between the leading men on both sides of the river with the purpose of either consolidating the two villages into one city, or come to some agreement. The negotiations were broken off as the parties could not agree on anything. Each side started a deputation to Columbus to procure a city charter. To the mortification of many of the east side, the people across the river had received their charter for the organization of Ohio City before the city of Cleveland came to hand, and Ohio City, therefore, took precedence in point of age. This embittered the jealous rivalry between the two cities, and produced a state of feeling which led to the "Battle of the Bridge," in 1837.

In 1835 Mr. James S. Clark built at his own expense, the old Columbus Street Bridge, connecting Cleveland with Brooklyn. When finished he devoted this bridge to public use. In 1837, after both the two cities had received their charters, both sides. claimed jurisdiction. From formal claims and council resolutions, the contestants proceeded to stronger measures. Each city sent armed men to take possession of the structure. A field piece was posted on the low ground on the east side, to rake the bridge. Weapons and missiles of all kinds were freely used on both sides, and many persons were wounded, some seriously. The draw was cut away, the middle pier and the western abutment partially blown down, and the field piece spiked by the west siders. The sheriff of the county and the city marshal of Cleveland at last appeared on the scene, gained possession of the dilapidated bridge, which had been given to Cleveland, and lodged some of the rioters in the county jail. The remainder of the battle was fought in the courts.

In 1851 the first railway was formally opened—the Cleveland, Columbus and Cincinnati, followed in rapid succession by the Lake Shore and Cleveland & Pittsburgh, and a little later by the lines to Toledo and down the Mahoning Valley. These opened up a new territory to the trade of the city, stimulated manufactures, and laid the foundation of the great prosperity it now enjoys. March 1st. 1880, the first train over the VALLEY RAILWAY entered Cleveland. This road runs from Canton to Cleveland, traversing the vast coal fields of the region. The road follows the course of the Cuyahoga River and enters Cleveland near the Standard Oil Works, at the corner of Broadway and Jefferson Streets, and follows along through the old canal bed to Seneca Street, where the present depot is located. Thus Cleveland now has six lines of railroads coming in from all directions, which makes it one of the great railroad centers of the world. The population of Cleveland, according to the United States census, was in 1830, 1,075 ; in 1850, 17,034 ; in 1870, 92,829 ; and in 1880, 160,000.

~AKRON~

SHIRT FACTORY!

Fine Goods a Specialty.

MANUFACTURE ONLY FROM MEASURE.

Forms for Self-Measurement Sent by Mail on Application.

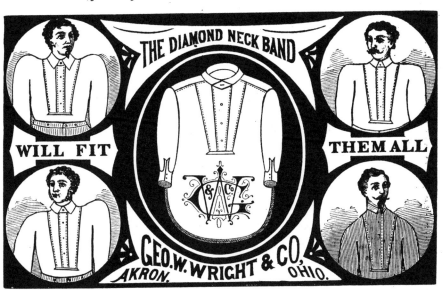

INVENTORS AND ONLY MANUFACTURERS OF THE

DIAMOND NECK BAND,

Which Fits All Shapes and Forms.

GEO. W. WRIGHT & CO.,

AKRON OHIO.

PUBLIC PARKS AND CEMETERIES.

CLEVELAND is unsurpassed in the number and beauty of her public parks, cemeter-teries, etc. We give a list of everything that would be of interest to the many visitors to the city.

Monumental Park, or Public Square, is situated in the center of the city. It is crossed by Superior and Ontario Streets. When the plan of Cleveland was first laid out, provisions were made for the accommodation of the future townsmen on public occasions, by setting apart ten acres in the center of the town as a Public Square. It was used for a long time as a play-ground for the village boys and a cow's pasture. On the 10th of September, 1860, the anniversary of the battle of Lake Erie, the marble statue of Commodore Perry, which now graces the center of the park, was unveiled with great ceremony, in the presence of one hundred thousand people. In the afternoon a representation of the battle took place on the Lake immediately off the city, the banks being thronged with spectators. The statue is eight feet and two inches in height, and stands on a pedestal of Rhode Island granite, the whole height, including the base, being twenty-five feet. The sculptor was William Walcutt, and all the work upon it was done in Cleveland. On the front of the pedestal is a circular tablet bearing an alto-relievo representing the passage of Perry in a boat from the disabled Lawrence to the Niagara in the midst of the fight. The monument is flanked by figures in marble of a sailor boy and a young midshipman. Several years ago the name of Public Square was changed to Monumental Park. The park is well shaded with elm and maple trees, and walks are laid out all through it with seats along the sides for the weary traveler to rest. In the north-west and south-west quarter are large fountains with ponds around them, the banks of which are fringed with beautiful flowers. In the center of the park are two war trophies, a cannon captured from the British at the battle of Lake Erie, and a field piece captured by the Cleveland Light Artillery at Carrick's Ford, West Virginia, in the war of the rebellion. In 1876, sub-scriptions were taken up to replace the old flag pole which had been blown down the year before. On the Fourth of July, 1876 the pole was raised with appropriate exercises. The new pole is one hundred and sixty feet high, the upper section of sixty feet being of wood, and the lower is composed of Bessemer Steel three-eighths of an inch thick, rolled in plates and riveted together so as to form a hollow cylinder. The steel pole weighs about six tons. The bottom rests on a Berea stone block ten feet square and one foot thick, and is eleven feet under ground. To a heavy iron collar on the pole near the base is fastened two large braces, making it perfectly safe and secure. Upon this collar are medallions bearing the dates 1776 and 1876, interlaced with each other and surrounded by the in-scription "United we stand ; divided we fall," and "The flag of the Union forever."

Lake View Park, occupies the lake front of the city from Seneca Street eastward to Erie Street. This is one of the most attractive spots to be found anywhere in the shape of a public park. It is laid out with walks, grass plats, fountains, rustic seats, and com-mands a full view of the lake, and the tracks of the L. S. & M. S. and the C. &. P. Rail-roads, which run along the shore of the lake before entering the Union Depot, which is near the western end of the park.

The Circle, is an open space on the west side, on Franklin Street, from which Han-over and other streets radiate. It is ornamented with shade trees and a fountain, with seats distributed along the walks for the accommodation of the public.

Clinton Park is a place on Lake Street, surrounded by Clinton Court, which is hand-somely shaded with trees and kept in good order for the accommodation of the residents of that part of the city.

Erie Street Cemetery, is the oldest now in existence in the city. The land of this cemetery, ten acres in extent, was given to the settlement in 1808 by the Connecticut

Company, under whose auspices the town was laid out and settled.   The grounds are laid out in twelve sections, containing from two to three hundred lots in each section. The main avenue is heavily shaded with trees, and well grown trees are scattered over the entire space.   Many tombs and monuments are of striking and tasteful designs.   The receiving vault, situated in the east center, is ten by twenty-four feet, mostly beneath the surface, and entered by an arch.   The cemetery is now so crowded that no interments are permitted except in lots already owned by the representatives of the deceased.   Many bodies previously interred there have been removed by friends to the other and newer cemeteries.

Woodland Cemetery, is situated on the north side of Woodland Avenue, between Cemetery and Giddings Avenues, about one mile from Monumental Park.   It contains sixty acres of land, beautifully laid out and well filled with monuments, tomb-stones and other memoriums of the dead.   The main entrance is on Woodland Avenue, through a

PUBLIC SQUARE, NORTH-WEST SECTION, 1880.—(See page 39.)

handsome Gothic gateway, erected in 1870 at a cost of about $8,000.   The gateway is flanked by a chapel and waiting room, tastefully arranged.   The receiving vault is a little to the east of the main entrance.   In the center of the grounds is a spacious and handsome pavillion, commanding a view of a large portion of the grounds.

Monroe Street Cemetery is on Monroe Street, west side, between Green and Jersey Streets.   It is handsomely laid out in drives and walks which are kept in good order.   In the south end of the grounds is the receiving vault, a Gothic building eighteen by twenty-four feet, the interior of which is arranged on an entirely new plan for handling caskets.

Lake View Cemetery, is on Euclid Avenue, beyond the city limits, in the village of East Cleveland, being about five miles from Monumental Park.   The grounds occupy three hundred and four acres, and are tastefully and artistically laid out in lots, and contains many costly monuments.

Riverside Cemetery, consists of about one hundred acres, and is about three miles from Monumental Park, just north of the junction of Scranton Avenue and the old Columbus road.

Catholic Cemetery is on the south side of Woodland Avenue, between Geneva Street and Giddings Avenue, nearly opposite Woodland Cemetery.

St. Mary's Cemetery is on the East side of Burton Street, corner of Clark Avenue.

Jewish Cemeteries are on Siam Street, betweet Willet and Japan Streets.

CHURCHES.

A view of the city from the distance reveals the existence of so many church edifices, that it might properly be called the city of churches. There is now over one hundred and thirty-five churches in all, so it would be impossible to locate them in this volume, but we will give the number of each denomination, and locate a few of the principal ones. They are classified as follows :—Methodist Episcopal, 20 ; Protestant Episcopal, 14 ; Roman Catholic, 21 ; Congregational, 11 ; Presbyterian, 9 ; Reformed, 6 ; Evangelical Association, 6 ; United Evangelical, 3 ; Evangelical Lutheran, 3 ; Hebrew, 3 ; Christian, 3 ; Evangelical Protestant, 2 ; Bible Christian, 2 ; Spiritualists, 2 ; United Brethren, 2 ; Universalist, 2 ; Free Will Baptist, 1 ; Society of Friends, 1 ; Swedenborgian, 1 ; Bethel Union, 1 ; etc., etc.

The principal churches are:—The Trinity (Episcopal) Superior Street, opposite Bond Street ; St. Pauls on Euclid Avenue, corner Case Avenue ; the First Methodist Episcopal Church, corner Euclid Avenue and Erie Street ; the First Presbyterian Church is located at the corner of Monumental Park and Ontario Street ; the First Baptist at the corner of Euclid Avenue and Erie Street ; St. Joseph's Church (Roman Catholic) at the corner of Woodland Avenue and Chapel Streets, is a grand Structure, under charge of the Franciscan Monks, whose convent is at the corner of Chapel and Hazen Streets.

SCHOOLS.

No feature of Cleveland is a source of more pride on the part of the citizens than the Public Schools. They are known to educators all over the Union as ranking among the highest, and visitors from all parts have borne testimony to their excellence. There are nearly forty public schools in different parts of the city, located for the convenience of the public. The principal buildings are the Central High School, Euclid Avenue between Erie and Sheriff ; East High School, Bolton Avenue, between Euclid and Cedar Avenues ; West High School, State Street corner of Ann ; Normal School, Eagle Street between Woodland Avenue and Erie. In addition to the free schools, there are over forty Catholic, private and mission schools in various parts of the city.

VARIOUS INSTITUTIONS.

THE CLEVELAND PUBLIC LIBRARY is located in the City Hall Building on the north side of Superior Street, corner of Wood Street. There are over twenty-five thousand volumes on its shelves, and the use of all parts of the library is free to every resident of the city.

THE WESTERN RESERVE AND NORTHERN OHIO HISTORICAL SOCIETY, occupies the entire third floor of the building of the Society for Savings, at the north-east corner of Monumental Park. It has the finest museum in the west, and a large library of scientific books.

THE NORTHERN OHIO HOSPITAL FOR THE INSANE is a large and fine building surrounded with attractive grounds, and is well worth visiting. It is located in the eastern part of the city, near the C. &. P. R. R. track.

THE YOUNG MEN'S CHRISTIAN ASSOCIATION building is located on the north side of Monumental Park. It includes a chapel, reading and music rooms, parlors, committee rooms, and a kitchen for use when social receptions are given. In the rear of the building is the structure known as the Newsboys' and Bootblacks' Home.

THE FRIENDLY INNS are four in number, three being on the east side and one on the west side, on Pearl Street. The principal establishment is at Central Place, where ample rooms and excellent accommodations are provided. Another on St. Clair Street, and a third on River Street. These places are well supplied with books and papers that are free to all. Prayer meetings are held at these places nearly every evening during the week.

THE BETHEL UNION is on the corner of Superior and Union Streets. It has a fine reading room and a cheap eating room, and a dining room for ladies and business men.

THE CITY HALL is on the north side of Superior Street, corner of Wood Street. It was built by Leonard Case, and completed in February, 1875, and in that month it was leased to the city for twenty-five years, at an annual rental of $36,000, the value of the property being estimated at $800,000. The edifice has a front of 217 feet on Superior Street, and is five stories high beside a basement under the whole. The first floor is divided into eight fine stores. On each of the second, third and fourth floors are sixteen complete suites of rooms, forty-eight suites in all, each suite consisting of two large rooms and three closets. The Council Chamber is on the highest floor, twenty feet in height, with a gallery for spectators. A steam elevator connects all the floors. In this building are gathered all the city offices except the water works office, which is in Cushing's Block, at the junction of Euclid Avenue and Monumental Park. The location of the several offices are as follows:—On the ground floor fronting the entrance, is the reading room. On the first floor are the offices of the Mayor, City Treasurer, City Solicitor and his assistants, Health Officer, Secretary of the Board of Health, Board of Improvements, Fire Commissioner, Board of Police and Public Library. The second floor is occupied by the Park Commissioners, City Auditor, City Clerk, and Public Library. On the third floor are the City Civil Engineer and his assistants, the remainder of the upper part of the building being taken up with the Council Chamber.

THE COURT HOUSE is on Seneca Street corner Frankfort. The building is of stone, and is not quite completed. When the north and south wings are finished it will be one of the finest buildings in the city.

THE CUSTOM HOUSE AND POST OFFICE is located in the United States Building on the east side of Monumental Park, north of Superior Street.

THE WORK HOUSE is a large fine building situated on Woodland Avenue, at the crossing of the C. & P. Railroad.

THE VIADUCT is one of the great improvements the city has received in the past eight years. Work was commenced on this immense structure in October, 1874, and was completed a few years ago. It connects the two sides of the river by crossing the river valley from bank to bank. It extends from the Atwater Block on the east side, to the junction of Detroit and Pearl Streets on the west side, crossing the valley of the Cuyahoga about 68 feet above the river. It is about 3,200 feet long and 64 feet wide. The river is crossed by a draw-bridge 330 feet long. We give an excellent illustration of the viaduct taken from the east side and showing the draw open. The cost of this structure was about $2,500,000.

EUCLID AVENUE OPERA HOUSE is on the corner of Euclid Avenue and Sheriff Streets, and is one of the finest and best appointed places of amusement in the United States. The main entrance is on Euclid Avenue through a vestibule 40 feet wide.

THE VIADUCT FROM ATWATER BLOCK, CLEVELAND.—(See page 48.)

7

CASE HALL stands on Superior Street, east of Monumental Park, and between the Government Building and the City Hall. It is one of the finest halls in the west, and is devoted mostly to lectures and concerts. Its seating capacity is 1,328.

ACADEMY OF MUSIC, Bank Street, between Superior and St. Clair.

GLOBE THEATRE at 205 Superior Street, is chiefly used for minstrel and concert troupes.

THEATRE COMIQUE, Frankfort Street near Bank Street, is the oldest theatre in the city, and is open all the year round as a variety theatre.

UNION PASSENGER DEPOT is situated on the lake shore, at the foot of Bank and Water Streets.

NEW YORK, PENNSYLVANIA AND OHIO PASSENGER DEPOT is on Scranton Avenue near the junction of Jennings Avenue.

PERRY'S MONUMEMT.
(See page 42.)

VALLEY RAILWAY DEPOT AND FREIGHT HOUSE is at the foot of Seneca Street.

THE CLEVELAND PAPER COMPANY have two mills sitated on the line of the VALLEY RAILWAY. The Valley Paper Mill is located at the mouth of Burke Brook, between the Ohio Canal and the Cuyahoga River. The connection with the city is made by a steamboat owned by the Company, which transports stock 'to and from the city. The Broadway Mill is located at the intersection of the N. Y. P. & O. R. R., and the VALLEY RAILWAY near the Standard Oil Works.

BROOKLYN.

THE village of Brooklyn is situated on the line of the VALLEY RAILWAY four and one-half miles south of Cleveland. The village was laid out in part, in the year 1830, by Moses Fish, an early settler and the owner of considerable land in what is now the center of the village. Although the village began thus early to push itself into notice, it was

not incorporated until August 5, 1867. Brooklyn village is now a thriving place of about fifteen hundred inhabitants, contains many fine residences and has some important manufacturing establishments. In the year 1840, Moses Merill, a New York school teacher happened to visit Brooklyn about the time its prominent citizens were agitating the subject of starting an academy. They secured Merill to teach for them ; put up a frame building on the lot now occupied by the Brooklyn village school. They called it the Brooklyn Academy and opened it as a select school of some pretentions. It flourished for several years as an important institute of learning, but gave way eventually before the rapid strides of the public school system, and disappeared. The old academy building is now used in part, for the village post-office. Brooklyn township joins the city of Cleveland on the west and south. It included originally all that part of the city of Cleveland lying on the west side of the Cuyahoga River. It contains four villages : Brooklyn, Brighton, West Cleveland and Lindale.

BRIGHTON.

The village of Brighton is five miles south of Cleveland, and near the VALLEY RAILWAY (Passengers for this station get on and off at Brooklyn station). The village was laid out originally upon land occupied by Warren Young's farm, and additional surveys were made from time to time. Its progress is unmarked by special incident until 1836, when, under the influence of the energy of Samuel H. Barstow, matters began to look up. Speculation in lots began to grow in earnest, and to further stimulate the spirit of the hour, Mr. Barstow procured the incorporation of the village. At the first election, early in 1837, twenty-three votes were cast for Mayor, Nathan Babcock receiving fourteen and Samuel H. Barstow nine. A. S. Palmer was chosen as Recorder, and a Mr. Clemens as Marshal and Street Commissioner. In less than a year, however, Brighton came to a standstill. When the next election time came the villagers concluded that the new departure was a failure and declined to hold an election, and the charter went to default. Since that time the progress of Brighton has been slow, yet in all it has been considerable. It has a population of about eight hundred, and is abundantly supplied with stores and hotels, has three churches and does a small business in the manufacture of wagons. The villagers are mostly Germans. An academy was founded here in 1840 but soon failed.

INDEPENDENCE.

THIS is the only village in Independence Township and is sometimes called the Center. It is situated eleven miles south of Cleveland on the line of the VALLEY RAILWAY, the village is situated one and one-fourth miles west of the depot. The village is situated on the State road, and located on an elevated plateau which slopes south-west towards Hemlock Creek. (The VALLEY ROAD crosses this creek near the depot). At present it presents a somewhat scattered appearance, and is composed mainly of humble homes of those who find employment outside the village. It contains a Roman Catholic, a Presbyterian, and an Evangelical Church, a fine school house, the town hall and about four hundred inhabitants. The chief industry of Independence, besides the agricultural pursuits, is the quarrying of stone. West of the river the surface is underlaid by a ledge of superior sandstone, the composition of which is so fine that it makes the very best of grindstones. To quarry and manufacture these gives employment to hundreds of men and constitutes a business of more than $500,000 per year. Most of the products have been shipped to Cleveland by canal, but now, the VALLEY RAILWAY carries considerable of it.

BRECKSVILLE.

The village of Brecksville is situated on the south bank of Chippewa Creek, near the center of Brecksville Township, Cuyahoga County, usually called Brecksville Center. It is sixteen miles from Cleveland on the line of the VALLEY RAILWAY. The railroad crosses Chippewa Creek at the Hog Back. The village is two miles from the depot and is the only village in the Township. It is pleasantly located and contains the town hall, a very handsome school building, a Presbyterian and a Methodist Church, several stores and a number of very fine residences. For the past eight years a cheese

CITY HALL, CLEVELAND.—(See page 48.)

factory has been in successful operation, and this and the mills constitute the only manufacturing interests of the Township. It receives its name from Robert and John Breck, two of the proprietors who owned the land of the Township in common with several other parties. The soil varies from a stiff clay to a sandy loam, and is best adapted to grain and grasses, the latter being the principal product.

BOSTON.

The village of Boston is situated on the line of the VALLEY RAILWAY and the Ohio Canal, twenty miles south of Cleveland. Boston's greatest prosperity was between the years 1825 and 1842. It had first-class water power, a fine mill, a huge warehouse, two stores, a saloon, a hotel and a population of about three hundred inhabitants. The canal brought its business and patronage. Then it fell into the hands of parties who would neither manifest nor encourage enterprise. It died virtually, and its revival as a town is of but a comparatively recent date. Now with the advantages which the VALLEY RAIL- WAY will bring to it, the town will surely grow and prosper. About forty-five years ago, a band of counterfeiters were located here, known as the "Band of Secret Brothers." Counterfeit money was manufactured here in large quantities and carried on horseback by different members of the gang to the east, put in circulation, and the good money was brought back. But they have since been brought to justice and made to suffer the pen- alty of their crime. (The compiler of this book has in his possession some of the money that was manufactured here.) Up to about seventy-five years ago, near where the present depot stands was the headquarters of the Seneca Indians under their Chief Stigwanish, who erected a god of wood, to whom he paid his devotions, especially when he was about to go on his hunting and marauding expeditions.

On Friday, August 15, 1879, the track layers on the VALLEY RAILWAY reached Boston and the people all turned out to have a grand jollification. A train of four car loads came from Akron in the morning and by noon over 2,000 people were on the grounds. A grand pic-nic dinner was given for all present and a big supper was spread for the railroad laborers before the train left in the evening. There was music by the band, and the booming of the cannon when the train arrived. The ceremonies and pic- nic was held in the grove in front of the depot, which was nicely decorated with flags, some of the flag staffs are still standing. Part of the morning and afternoon was de- voted to speaking by many eminent men and pioneers of the valley. The welcome ad- dress was delivered at eleven A. M., by H. V. Bronson, a pioneer of Peninsula. We publish the address in full, which is very interesting and worthy of space in this book.

"LADIES AND GENTLEMEN :—In behalf of the citizens of this town, I tender you a cordial welcome. Preliminary to the address to be delivered on this occasion, I propose to say a few words on the past, present and future. History reveals the fact that civili- zation, progress, the arts and sciences have far exceeded during the four-fifths of the nineteenth century now at its close, the whole of the preceding time that we have of the history of this earth, and the continent of North America leads the van in that progress. Seventy-five years ago and previous to that time, this immediate vicinity was the head- quarters of Ponty, chief of an Indian tribe, and the residence of that pious devoted red man Stigwanish, who within a few rods of this, erected a wooden god, to whom he paid his devotions, especially when about to go on his hunting and marauding expeditions. Jonas Stanord, in 1806, settled within a short distance of this spot where his son John- son was born, being the first white child born in the township, in 1807, and he now re- sides in Hancock County in the western part of this State, and George Stanford, his old- est brother who is now 79 years old, has lived on the same farm, in sight of this spot for the past 73 years, and who is now here to celebrate with us on this occasion. From 40 to 42 years ago, this place was the headquarters of an association of men engaged in an illegitimate occupation. At the latter date they abruptly took their departure. Some were fugitives from justice, some paid service in penal servitude for violated law, and some sleep the sleep that knows no waking, under the sod in yonder beautiful cemetery, the most beautiful location for that purpose in Northern Ohio. They made history, and have proved that the way of the transgressor is hard ; unfortunately for the locality, lay- ing aside the law as handed down from Sinai, and applying it only in a human way, the sins of the father are visited upon the children. On the 12th. of June last, it was 55 years ago that the Ohio Canal was located from Cleveland south up the Cuyahoga valley. On the 4th. of July last, 52 years ago, the canal was formally opened as a channel of com- merce from Cleveland to Akron. About 15 years ago, the subject of building a railway in this valley was being agitated. Eight years ago, a company was charted for that pur- pose. Seven years ago it was surveyed and located. Six years ago the 26th of March

last, work was commenced, but in consequence of financial difficulties work was suspended. About one year ago work was resumed, and to-day we have met to welcome the long-looked-for locomotive, and we have a right to meet and rejoice. The VALLEY RAILWAY is destined to be one of the most important public improvements in Ohio, for the locality through which it passes, is independent of other roads, and intended to be kept so ; and from a personal knowledge of the topography of the country from Cleveland to the great coal, ore, fire and potter clay, lime-stone and sand-stone, in Northern and Central Ohio, no other route can possibly be found where the mineral region can be reached from the great chain of lakes, with slighter grades and shorter distances, than the VALLEY RAILWAY ; where fuel, ores, and pure soft water can be had either on a level or down hill, and Cleveland, the Cuyahoga and Tuscarawas valleys are destined to be the cheapest locations for manufacturing purposes in the United States, where the raw and manufactured article can be got to and from those localities to the civilized world. With these few brief remarks, I again extend a cordial welcome to all."

PENINSULA.

This pleasant village is situated in Boston Township, Summit County, twenty-two miles south of Cleveland, on the line of the VALLEY RAILWAY, which runs directly through the village. The name is derived from the peculiar course of the river as it runs through the village, making three distinct peninsulas as will be seen by the map below.

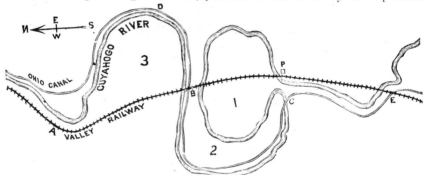

EXPLANATION OF MAP.

Nos. 1, 2 and 3 are the peninsulas; P, Peninsula depot : A. Great Bend on the VALLEY ROAD; B, "Devil's Passage," (see page 12) : C, is where the canal crosses the river through an aqueduct; D, the ice houses of the Lake Erie Ice Company ; E, where the river and canal are crossed by the VALLEY ROAD near the stone quarry

The river flows from the south, placid, quietly and dignifiedly and straight, through the midst of the village till it arrives at the point where the VALLEY RAILWAY depot is, when it suddenly takes a turn to the east and flows around twenty acres of land and coming back to within sixteen feet of itself again ; thus forming peninsula number one. It then flows west and then east, coming around the hill and appearing at the north end of the Devil's Passage, marked B on the map ; thus forming peninsula number two, which contains fifty acres. It flows around the low flat and appears again at the Great Bend of the VALLEY RAILWAY, marked A on the map ; this makes peninsula number three, containing thirty acres. The point marked P is the depot of the VALLEY RAILWAY at Peninsula village. The railroad runs directly across peninsula number one. This would have necessitated the building of two bridges within half a mile, but the railroad adopted a more ingenious and economical plan. Cutting through the narrow isthmus the width

8

of the river bed opposite the depot, and damming up the old channel, the course of the river was entirely changed and now it runs off to the west and passes under the canal aqueduct without going around peninsula number one—which is no more a peninsula. The railroad crosses where the dams were made, and all the expenses of building two bridges was dispensed with.

Peninsula is a beautiful city of about 700 inhabitants, and was first settled in the year 1810. It contains two hotels, a number of stores, several saw-mills, one grist mill, two

BIG NARROWS, 2½ MILES NORTH OF AKRON.—(See page 16.)

churches and good schools. It is a tying-up place for a good many canal boats, and her population is made up somewhat of canal men. Quite an extensive business was carried on in boat building until the year 1870. In consequence of the dilapidated condition of the canal no boats have been built here for the past ten years. There are two good and permanent water-powers on the river, one of seven feet fall and the other eight feet. The Peninsula stone quarries extend along the southern part of the village on the west side of the river. The stone work at the Water Works Crib of Cleveland is built of Peninsula stone. The scenery about the town is wild and romantic in many localities.

EVERETT.

This pleasant little village is situated on the banks of the Ohio Canal and on the line of the Valley Railway, twenty-four and three-fourths miles south of Cleveland, the railroad passing through the village. The village is very old, having been settled in 1826, at the time of the building of the Ohio Canal, but has grown very little since. It

E. I. BALDWIN & CO.,

214 and 216 Superior Street,

CLEVELAND, OHIO.

The firm of E. I. Baldwin & Co. is the oldest retail *Dry Goods* establishment in Northern Ohio, and has for more than twenty years controlled the largest trade in this line. Possessed of ample means to take advantage of European and American markets, they exhibit a stock unequaled in extent, quality and cheapness. The building in which their business is conducted, Nos. 214 and 216 Superior street, is a model of convenience, and adapted to the distribution of a million dollars worth of goods per annum. On the main floor are *Silks* of all grade and styles, from fifty cents to twelve dollars per yard; *Velvets*, plain and brocade; *Dress Goods* of every conceivable design; Dress Trimmings and Buttons; *Laces* and Embroideries; *Kid Gloves*, Fabrique Gloves, Hosiery and Under-wear; Woolen Goods for men; Ladies' Cloakings and Suiting Cloths; Flannels and Cottons; Gents' Furnishing Goods; Umbrellas, White Goods, Notions, Ginghams, Prints, etc.

Taking the elevator, one is lifted in a moment to the second floor, a very fine sales-room, forty-two by one hundred and sixty feet, lighted by an immense dome light, where are exhibited *Cloaks and Suits* for ladies and children; *Shawls* of more than eight hundred varieties; *Linens, Blankets, Quilts* and other goods for housekeepers; Ladies' and Infants' Cambric wear, etc.

The next floor presents the most complete line of *Curtain Goods* and Curtains, India and American Rugs, Floor Oil Cloths, Druggets and Door Mats. Here are also Cretonnes, Damasks, Raw Silks, Cashmeres, Reps, Chintzes, etc., for furniture, upholstery and curtain purposes.

Throughout the store of Messrs. E. I. Baldwin & Co. one notices the perfect system by which the business is conducted; so that notwithstanding the small army of clerks and the great number of customers, everything moves satisfactorily. This establishment was the first Western house to introduce the *one price system* and to maintain strictly cash transactions.

It may be also a matter of interest to refer to the politeness and courtesy of the clerks employed in this house, who appear never to weary in their efforts to serve the numerous patrons.

has about one hundred inhabitants, two stores, a school house, hotel and livery stable. It has always been known as "Johnny Cake Lock," which name it received when the canal was being built. The laborers here received Johnny cake as their chief article of food. It was afterward changed by the railroad to Unionville, but has since been changed to Everett, in honor of S. T. Everett, Treasurer of the Valley Railway.

The following anecdote, in relation to the former name of the village, may not be out of place. Many years ago, before railroads were discovered, or tramping was invented, when people thought it more aristocratic to go by canal boat than to go afoot, the staunch A No. 1 clipper ship, "Samantha Ann," becalmed on the waste of waters west of Akron, owing to the forward mule casting a shoe, and laming itself by stepping into a chuckhole on the tow-path, and there balking, refused to go. For nearly forty-eight hours were the passengers exposed to the scorching sun as the Samantha Ann lay as "idle as a painted ship upon a painted ocean." Provisions got low, the last flip of bacon had been fried, the last ship's biscuit had gone by the board(ers), and things looked desperate. They were on the point of casting lots to see which of their number should be eaten (a very lean and very much dried up old gentleman being barred from the contest), when the forward mule pooled his grievances, and, in consideration of two ears of corn slung six inches in front of his nose by a stick between his ears, agreed to go forward. They weighed anchor and moved upon their way. Provisions were low, but there was a little hamlet ahead where relief could be found. They reached it, and the famished passengers made a rush for the houses. At each house they were offered nothing but Johnny cake, so they went no further, but loaded their boat up with slabs of "Johnny cake," like wood, and as they sailed out of that town the passengers stood in indignation, meeting in the stern of the boat, and gazing in amazement at the receding hamlet, said: "Henceforth it shall be called 'Johnny Cake,'" and it was. It is evident that the inhabitants are corn-bred.

BOTZUMS.

This small village is situated on the Ohio Canal, and on the line of the Valley Railway, twenty-eight miles south of Cleveland. Its greatest prosperity was during the early times of the canal. A large warehouse and a store, with about a dozen houses, constitutes the place. It has formerly been known as Niles, or Yellow Creek, but the railroad company changed it to Botzum's.

A short distance north of the depot the railroad passes between two mounds supposed to have been built many centuries ago by the race before the Indians, called the Mound Builders. The mound on the left is small and round, with a tall tree on the top; the one on the right is large and square shaped, and about fifteen feet high, out in the open field. Just north of the depot the road passes through the old Indian or Mound Builders' burying ground. The following, taken from a history of Summit County, published in 1854, shows what this place looked like then: "This extensive grave yard is covered with a forest of a growth as large as the surrounding woods, and its size and number of graves, prove it to be the final resting place of an immense population. Crockery of a good quality has been taken from the graves, but nothing to fix the date of this ancient people. All we know is that they once existed; their works prove that they were almost numberless; their fortifications show them to have been warlike; their burial mounds are monuments of their desire to have their names, deeds and memories, handed down to posterity. But this evidence of their desire is all that remains. They are forgotten and their history is unknown."

INMAN BROS.,

No. 184 EAST MARKET STREET, East Akron, Ohio.

The foundation of this establishment was laid immediately after the close of the rebellion, by the senior partner, Mr. Fred. W. Inman. Previous to this time this gentleman had been in the medical profession and had served in that capacity through the war. Finding that this occupation was not in harmony with his temperament and abilities, he abandoned it for a more active business life. He bought a half interest in the store of his father-in-law, Dr. M. Jewett. This firm was known by the name of Jewett & Inman, and paid their attention to the drug and grocery trade. After one or two changes in the firm, at the end of two or three years Mr. Inman found himself sole proprietor. The establishment was then situated at the corner of Market and Water streets. The next change in the firm was the admission of Mr. Sid. C. Inman, who had heretofore been connected with the house as junior partner, the firm then bearing the name of F. W. Inman & Bro., which has since been changed to Inman Brothers.

In 1873, finding that their business had so much increased that it could not be accommodated in their present quarters, they erected a fine brick business block immediately across the Little Cuyahoga from their old stand. This building, though large and finely adapted to the business, was not sufficiently large to accommodate their steadily increasing trade, and in 1879 they were obliged to build their present magnificent warehouse. This is one of the finest structures for the purpose named that can be found in this or any other section. These two buildings constitute their present business block, which is apartmented and used in the following manner: The front building is one hundred feet by twenty-six feet, three story and basement high. The basement of this part is used for storing oils, vinegars, paints, packed meats and wet goods of various kinds. The first floor is the general sale room of the house, this being one hundred feet by twenty-five feet. The second story is divided into dwelling apartments and offices. The third floor is the finely fitted hall of the Apollo Lodge, I. O. O. F. This completes the front building. The warehouse is forty by forty-six feet and the same heighth as the other building, three story and basement. The basement is used for packing purposes, as the firm, in winter season, engage heavily in pork packing and ham curing. Their productions in this line are procuring them quite a wide-spread reputation. The second floor is for general warehouse purposes, with the exception of one apartment, which is the cooling room of one of Fisher's finest Chicago refrigerators. This was put up at quite an expense to the firm—is eighteen by twenty feet. The ice used for the cooling of this room occupies the same part of the second floor. The capacity of the ice room is eighty ton, which is filled in the winter, colling the room below until the coming winter. This enables them to supply their trade, through the hot summer season, with the finest and freshest vegetables, produce and meats of all kinds that the market can afford. The remainder of the second floor is used for dry drug storage and dry paints.

The third floor is used for storing cement, salt, feed and surplus stock. The stock carried by this firm is from ten to twelve thousand dollars. From five to six clerks are employed and two delivery wagons run. The firm do a large business, outside of their general trade, by handling corn, potatoes, apples, etc., in large shipments by canal and railroad.

OLD PORTAGE.

From the beginning of the present century up to 1830, Old Portage was one of the great towns of Northern Ohio. It was the head of navigation on the Cuyahoga River. Now only three houses remain of that once flourishing village. The idea has of late years been instituted in the public mind, that some of the vessels used by Commodore Perry in his battle on Lake Erie was built at this place, which is not so. Some of the timber of his fleet was taken from the forests in this vicinity and rafted down the river to Cleveland. From there they were taken to Erie, Pa., where the vessels were built. Some of the pine for spars was got in the pinery on the east side of the river from Brecksville depot on the VALLEY RAILWAY. The craft on the Cuyahoga River at that time was small, carrying only six or eight tons.

CITY OF AKRON.

The thriving, enterprising city of Akron, is the county seat of Summit County, and is located on the highest ground in the State, being 495 feet above Lake Erie and 1,065 feet above the ocean. It is thirty-four and a half miles south of Cleveland on the line of the VALLEY RAILWAY. The city was laid out in 1825. Charles Olcott, a graduate of Yale College, and a Greek scholar, suggested the name *Akron*, which is a Greek word, signifying a peak, or summit, which was at once adopted. The ground on which it stands was purchased from the Indians at a treaty held at Fort McIntosh, where Beaver, Pennsylvania, now stands, in 1785, by which the Cuyahoga River, the Portage Path, and Tuscarawas River were fixed upon as the western boundary of the United States. From 1785 to 1805 the site of Akron was the extreme limit of the United States, and from this frontier to the Pacific Ocean was an unbroken wilderness, and the only highway through this vast territory was an Indian trail. It seems almost incredible, but it is a fact nevertheless, that within three-quarters of a century all this thousands of miles of expanse has become thickly studded with populous cities and thriving towns, and where was formerly the solitary trail of the red man, speeds along the powerful locomotive, drawing its train of precious freight. Such is the wonderful story of human civilization and human progress.

The first settler in Portage township was Major Miner Spicer, who came from Groton, Connecticut, in 1810 and selected his land about midway between the original limits of Akron and what was then Middlebury (now Sixth Ward of Akron, and the East Akron station on the VALLEY RAILWAY). His son, Avery Spicer, now lives on their land. At that time there was not a road, a clearing, or a white person in the township. Having selected his land and made some improvements, he returned to Groton, Connecticut, for his family. In 1811, in company with his brothers Amos, and Paul, and Barnabas Williams, he came back to his wilderness home. Paul Williams located a little west of Major Spicer, on what is now called Exchange street, a little west of the present location of Buchtel College.

In September, 1825, ground was broken for the Ohio Canal, a little north of what is now Lock 1, in the southern part of Akron, it having been commenced at Licking Summit on the 4th of July previous. Immediately after the location of the canal, General Simon Perkins and Paul Williams laid out Akron, and platted it, and recorded it as a village. In what was then the recorded plat, there were but two families—Paul and Barnabas Williams. The first house erected in Akron, as it was then laid out, was in the year 1825, on the corner of Exchange and Main streets; it was two stories high and was for many years occupied by C. P. McDaniels as a hotel. The timber of which it was constructed was cut from the ground where it stood. In 1827, Akron became a port, and Woolsey Wills, attorney at law, Justice of the Peace, and postmaster, was appointed Collector of the Port of Akron. On the 4th of July, 1827, the first canal boat left Akron for

WHERE SHALL WE BUY BOOKS?

The name of INGHAM, CLARKE & Co., of Cleveland, is so widely known to book lovers and book buyers it has become a "household word," during the eighteen years they have been established in business. Their main salesroom, at 217 Superior street, (opposite E. I. Baldwin & Co.'s Dry Goods Store), is 175 feet in length, and is crowded from floor to ceiling with Books and Stationery of every kind. It is the general resort of reading people, and is well worth anybody's visit to examine

WHAT KINDS THEY HAVE.

We specify a little, beginning with the department of *School Books and School Material*, which includes every school book used in Northern Ohio, and every other thing in supplies that a school can use. The *Law Department* is extremely full, this firm having expended ten thousand dollars in publishing a single work on Ohio law. *Medical Books* are abundant and the variety complete. From the *Sunday School Department* they have supplied over one million Sunday School Books, and they are now supplying, each month, over sixteen thousand papers and lesson leaves of various kinds to the schools of Ohio. They have for years represented in the West the leading religious publishing societies, keeping on their shelves a very great variety of Sunday School Books, from all reliable sources. There is not a thing that a Sunday School needs that is lacking, from the largest blackboard down to the smallest infant class ticket. Send for their full catalogues. The American Bible Society has its agency here, and the five cent Testament and the twenty-five cent Bible, and hosts of other kinds or sizes are in stock, including the English Teachers' Bibles. The *Juvenile Book Department* contains thousands of the brightest and prettiest bound books and picture books the country affords. *Agricultural Books* have their place in full variety.

MORE DEPARTMENTS.

The department of *Church and Sunday School Music Books* is very full, including Choir and Prayer Meeting Books, and editions of their own are taken of all the prominent Sunday school music books. The great Moody & Sankey meetings were supplied with "Gospel Hymns" by this house. *Foreign Books* are largely carried in stock and intimate relations are had with foreign houses, so that any book published abroad may be quickly gotten. Two thousand volumes of foreign antiquarian books are now shown. The *Stationery Department* includes Blank Books of all sizes; Letter Paper, etc., of all styles, qualities, shades and sizes. The last importation of Photo Albums from Germany was immense and the styles very lovely. The new patterns of Autograph Albums are more beautiful than any before made. Pocket Books, Gold Pens, and the various *etcetera*, are in full supply, including the new Stylographic or Fountain Pen.
Wholesale or retail customers can be sure of the best market rates.

A SPECIAL AGENCY.

The American Book Exchange, that makes books so cheap, have an agency here; and you can get Chambers' Cyclopedia complete for $7.50, in fifteen volumes, or Macaulay's England for $1.50, or Munchausen for five cents; Pilgrim's Progress for six cents, and many others as marvellously low. Send a stamp for a full catalogue.
The *Miscellaneous Department* is full to repletion of standard poems and histories. Standard novels and fiction, and any book that is advertised in any paper anywhere can be supplied by this house. The current subscription books, that are "never sold in book stores," are sold continually here, and frequently at reduced prices. Village reading clubs and all book buyers can be assured of finding lowest terms at the store of

INGHAM, CLARKE & CO.,

217 SUPERIOR ST., CLEVELAND.

Cleveland, causing great rejoicing as it moved off at the rate of three miles an hour through the Portage and Northampton hills. At this time Woolsey Wells, Major Mills, Joshua King, and Joseph Keeler, the last of whom kept a little log grocery on the bank of the canal north of the Summit House, then composed the business part of Akron. In 1832, Charles W. Howard, one of the most enterprising business men that ever lived in Akron, erected a building on the corner known as Hall's store, which was burned February, 1851. In honor of his enterprise the principal street was named after him, "Howard street." The town at that time contained about 600 inhabitants. This is now the great business street of the city. The population of Akron in 1860 was 3,700; in 1870, 10,253, and the census for the year 1880 gives it a population of 16,462. It had been estimated by many during the past year to be about 20,000, and many were disappointed at the result of the census.

BEACON BLOCK.—(See page 29.)

The gross receipts of the Akron Post-office entitled the city to a free delivery of mail matter by carriers, and arrangements were made, boxes put up in different parts of the city, and five regular carriers began on March 1st of the present year, to deliver the mail daily from house to house. As Akron is a place situated among the hills, this system is of very great convenience to the citizens in general.

The need of Water Works has been felt by the citizens of Akron for several years past, but nothing was done towards supplying the need until the Akron Water Works Company was formed, in July of the present year. The only way to get pure water, that could be used for drinking as well as other purposes, was to construct an artesian well, and locate a reservoir on the highest ground near the city. Sherbondy Hill, the highest point in Summit County, just south of the city limits at the end of Wooster Avenue, was chosen for the reservoir site, and the land purchased at once. On Thursday, July 29th, work was commenced on the top of the hill to excavate for the reservoir, which is to hold about 4,000,000 gallons. At the foot of the hill a well fifty feet in diameter is being dug, from which the water will be pumped up into the reservoir. Test wells have been made, and the assurance of an unexhaustible supply of pure spring water has been the result. Pipes are now being placed along the streets, and it will not be many months before the city of Akron will be supplied with pure water.

By the great destructive conflagrations of June and December, 1848, December,

9

1849, February, 1851, December, 1854, and April, 1855, the business portion of ancient Akron was laid in ruins; but like the Phœnix of old, the city has often arisen from its ashes to begin again. Modern Akron has also suffered very severely from the ravages of the fire fiend, by the conflagrations of December, 1856, March, 1857, March, 1869, April, 1872, and June, 1878. But from all these calamities, involving an aggregate loss of over $1,000,000, its recovery has been rapid, and to-day this enterprising city has few superiors in the beauty of its business structures and public and private edifices, or in the enterprise and prosperity of its inhabitants.

ACADEMY OF MUSIC, AKRON.—(See pages 61 and 76.)

The manufacturing interests of the city are of a greatly diversified nature, and of great extent, numbering among them some of the largest and most successful enterprises of their kind in the United States. Some of the principal manufacturing establishments of the city are represented in this book. Among them is the great Buckeye Mower and Reaper Works, Barber Match Factory, the Artificial Stone Works of Palmer & Pruner, which is a new industry recently started here, Whitman & Barnes Manufacturing Company, etc., etc. There is now three railroads passing through the city, the New York, Pennsylvania & Ohio, Cleveland, Mt. Vernon & Columbus railroads, and the VALLEY RAILWAY. This affords through communication to all parts of the country, and giving a chance for competition on the various lines, and insures minimum rates for

fare and freight. Few interior cities are more favorably situated in this regard, making Akron one of the best points in the country for manufacturing enterprises. The fine water power at this point is another noteworthy advantage. The principal water power is derived from Summit Lake, lying about one mile south of the city, and which is a mile long and a half mile wide. This beautiful lake receives its supply from numerous living springs in its bed. It is of great importance to the city and State, as it not only runs a large number of mills and factories, but furnishes a never-failing supply to the Ohio Canal.

We have now given as complete a history of the city of Akron as could be obtained, and we will now describe and give the location of the various places and points of interest for the convenience of visitors and the citizens generally.

PUBLIC PARKS AND CEMETERIES.

GRACE PARK is a beautiful plat of about ten acres in the northeastern part of the city, and is bounded by Perkins Street on the north, Park Street on the south, N. Y., P. & O. and C., Mt. V. & C. railroads on the east, and Prospect Street on the west. It was donated to the city by Mrs. Grace Perkins and has been named after her. It is a cool and shady place, ornamented with forest trees and is laid out in grass plats and walks, along which comfortable seats are placed for the accommodation of the public.

UNION PARK is a triangular open space of about six acres in the eastern part of the city, and is bounded on the north and west by Mill and College Streets, and on the south and east by Forge Street. It is ornamented with a few shade trees, but is not laid out in walks. It is sometimes called the "Three Cornered Park."

PLEASANT PARK is in the southern part of the city, at the corner of Thornton and Washington Streets.

SOUTH AKRON PARK is a pleasant, green spot, ornamented with trees and flowers, at the corner of Exchange and Bowery Streets, opposite the Bowery School House.

FOUNTAIN PARK, Fair Grounds, is about one mile east of the city. It occupies 52 acres of ground in the valley of the Cuyahoga, where the Austin Powder Mills were located before they blew up about fifteen years ago. The grounds are owned by the Summit County Agricultural Society. Permanent exhibition buildings, stock pens, etc., etc., have been erected for the regular annual fairs. There is also a fine half-mile track. An artificial lake and a large fountain has been placed inside the curve at the east end of the race track, and the Little Cuyahoga River runs directly through the grounds. The numerous springs along the sides of the valley affords a continual supply of pure water, which is distributed over the grounds through pipes. The exhibitions by this society have been successful, and the attendance on a single day has been as high as 25,000. The VALLEY RAILWAY crosses these grounds on a trestle 1,000 feet long and 40 feet high. (See frontispiece engraving.)

GLENDALE CEMETERY is at the west end of Glendale Avenue, about half a mile from the postoffice. It contains 100 acres, and is handsomely laid out in drives and walks, and is a charming spot, with its grand old forest trees and shrubbery, hills and dales, groves and drives, and its many magnificent monuments and tombs. A small stream runs through it and divides it in two sections. Down in the valley between the two parts is a cool and pleasant drive along side of which the stream has been dammed, and a small lake formed, upon the surface of which a beautiful white swan can be seen as it glides gently over the water. This lake and swan forms the chief attraction of the cemetery. During the summer months great numbers of people spend their Sunday afternoons in this beautiful spot. No visitor should leave the city without visiting this cemetery. On the left, just inside the main entrance on Glendale Avenue, is the elegant MEMORIAL CHAPEL, which was erected and dedicated in honor of Akron's fallen heroes

ROBERTS & WOOD,

Plumbers and Gas Fitters

41 Prospect St., Cleveland, O.

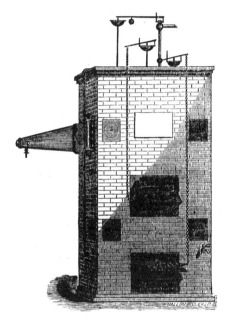 

IMPROVED

Automatic Low Pressure

STEAM

HEATING APPARATUS!

For Warming and Ventilating Private Residences, Public Buildings and Institutions, School Houses, Churches, Stores, Green Houses, &c.

PLUMBING, STEAM AND HOT WATER FITTING,

Done on the most approved plan, by experienced workmen at short notice.

Defects Remedied in Imperfectly Constructed Steam Heaters.

of the civil war. It is built on the cruciform plan, the nave being thirty feet wide by forty-eight feet long, and the width across at transepts being forty-eight feet, giving it an area of 1800 square feet on the ground. The foundations of stone are six feet broad, laid in cement. The beautiful arched entrance porch, with its enriched carved capitals, vases and cornice, is all of cut stone, except the six columns, which are of highly polished red granite. The inside walls are of dressed "constitution" stone, and the floor is covered with Milton tile. The entire structure, up to the roof line, is of masonry and iron, not a particle of any combustible or destructible material entering into its construction. Beneath the floor is the receiving vault, the entrance of which is at the rear of the Chapel. This elegant memorial edifice was dedicated on " Decoration Day," May 30th, 1876.

GERMAN CATHOLIC CEMETERY is on South Maple Street, adjoining Glendale Cemetery on the south. It is well filled with monuments, tombstones, and other memoriams of the dead. Many of the monuments are of costly design and workmanship.

CATHOLIC CEMETERY, west of Balch Street, near the city limits.

OLD CEMETERY, located on Newton Street, Sixth Ward. (East Akron.)

NEW SUMNER HOUSE, AKRON.—(See page 31.)

CHURCHES.

The moral community is well supplied with places of worship; lofty spires meet the eye in all directions as we draw near the city. Many of the church buildings are models of architectural beauty, handsomely decorated inside and out, and large sums have been expended in their erection. There are sixteen church edifices in the city, embracing all the different denominations, which are liberally supported and sustained by the community. We give the location of all the churches in the city:

FIRST M. E. CHURCH is on the corner of Broadway and Church streets. This is the finest and most tastefully arranged church edifice in the country. It was erected at a cost of over $140,000. The building is of brick, with stone trimmings, and has two lofty spires on the east portion of the structure. The whole building is heated by steam and lighted with gas. All of the windows are of beautifully designed stained glass. In front of the church is a beautiful green lawn, which is always kept neat and clean. A stone walk passes through it and branches to the two main doors of the church. This stately structure contains a main audience room, Sunday school room, lecture room, parlor,

library, pastors' study, and a kitchen, which is used when social receptions are given. The entrance to the main audience room is on Broadway. A gallery extends around the whole room, with the large and superb organ at the west end, which strikes the eye first upon entering. In front of this is the place for the choir; then a few feet below are the pulpits, which are two in number, upon a platform about five feet above the floor, and enclosed by a circular railing. The furniture, including the seats, is all of the finest walnut, richly finished. The walls and ceilings are very tastefully and appropriately frescoed. The arrangements for lighting and ventilating are of the most perfect character. Two large and elegant chandeliers are suspended from the ceiling, besides lights at all the posts under the gallery and at each end of the room. All these are lighted in an instant by electricity. The Sunday school room is so beautifully and tastefully arranged that it has been patterned after by many church organizations throughout the country. This room is arranged in a half circle, with a large and handsome fountain in the center. The scholars occupy chairs in the main room, and are divided into classes of seven scholars and a teacher. Each class has a desk around which they gather to study the lesson. Small rooms for the older scholars branch off from the main room, but they can all be opened into the large room where general exercises are going on. A gallery extends around half of the room, upon which class rooms open. Around the circle above the gallery, is the following inscription: "And they Searched the Scriptures Daily Whether those Things were So." The entrance to the Sunday school room is on Church Street. The Sunday school library contains a large number of interesting books.

FIRST UNIVERSALIST CHURCH is on the corner of Mill street and Broadway. It is one of the most striking buildings of the city, and was completed last year at a cost of $40,000. For beauty and design it will compare favorably with any similar structure in the country. It is built on the Medieval style, with circular towers, and handsomely decorated on the outside. The inside is finished in the Eastlake style in a very elaborate manner.

CONGREGATIONAL CHURCH is situated on High Street, between Market and Mill Streets. The town clock is on the dome of this church.

CHURCH OF CHRIST is on South High Street, between Mill and Quarry Streets.

TRINITY LUTHERAN CHURCH is on Prospect Street near Mill.

ST. PAUL'S EPISCOPAL CHURCH, on High Street near Mill.

FIRST BAPTIST CHURCH, east side of North High Street, between Market and Talmadge Streets.

GRACE REFORMED CHURCH, South Broadway near Mill Street.

EVANGELICAL ASSOCIATION CHURCH, southeast corner of Bartges and Coburn Streets.

AKRON HEBREW CONGREGATION hold their services on the third floor of 128 South Howard Street.

GERMAN LUTHERAN CHURCH, corner High and Quarry Streets.

GERMAN REFORMED CHURCH, corner Broadway and Center Streets.

ST. VINCENT DE PAUL'S CHURCH, (English Catholic) on the corner of West Market and Maple Streets.

ST. BERNARD'S CHURCH, (German Catholic) corner Broadway and Center Streets.

SECOND M. E. CHURCH, corner East High and Exchange Streets, Sixth Ward. (East Akron.)

PRESBYTERIAN CHURCH, East Market Street, Sixth Ward. (East Akron.)

SCHOOLS.

The public schools of Akron are not surpassed in the State for discipline and thoroughness. The system comprises three general departments—primary, grammar and

high school. The buildings are large, roomy, and provided with every improvement in construction, furniture, and educational appliances. There are twelve school buildings in different parts of the city, located for the convenience of the public.

The following is a list and location of the main buildings:

The CENTRAL SCHOOL BUILDING is on the corner of Mill and Summit streets. The play grounds extend from Summit to Prospect Street.

BROADWAY SCHOOL is on North Broadway.

PERKINS SCHOOL, corner Exchange and Bowery Streets.

SPICER SCHOOL is on Carroll, facing Short Street, a little east of Buchtel College.

Besides these, there are many smaller branch schools. There is also German and Catholic schools and several select schools in the city.

BUCHTEL COLLEGE is situated on Middlebury, opposite College Street. It is on the highest point of land in the State, and therefore commands a full view of the city and surrounding country. The building is 240 feet long, 54 feet wide, and five stories high. Its style of architecture combines, in artistic and symmetrical proportions, the Doric, Gothic and Norman. The building is furnished with modern and most improved conveniences, and is heated by steam and lighted by gas, and abundantly supplied with good water. The property is valued at $250,000.

VARIOUS INSTITUTIONS AND BUILDINGS.

AKRON PUBLIC LIBRARY is located in Masonic Block, on the northeast corner of Howard and Mill streets. This noble enterprise was incepted in the winter of 1867, by a few gentlemen, who decided that it would be a useful acquisition to the city. A plan was adopted, having in view the procuring of one hundred subscriptions at $50 each, entitling the subscribers to a life membership. The desired amount, $5,000, was soon obtained, and of this amount over $4,000 was invested in books, and the balance in furniture. In the following spring the library was opened, and the organization adopted rules admitting to membership residents, at $3 per year. Thus they continued until, by subscriptions and donations, they had accumulated books and other property to the value of $15,000, whereupon by vote of the life members, it was transferred entire to the city, upon conditions that it be accepted and made a free library, and that not less than $3,000 per year be expended in maintaining and increasing the collection. The terms were complied with, and the library continues to be well supported and is free to every resident of the city. The rooms are light, convenient, and well arranged, and contain over 7,000 volumes and is gradually increasing. A reading room is in connection with the library, which is supplied with many newspapers and periodicals of the day.

AKRON CITY MUSEUM adjoins the Public Library, and is under the auspices of the Akron Scientific Club. The museum contains many interesting specimens in natural history, relics, fossils, mounted birds, antiquities, etc., etc. It is open most all day and evening, and is free to all.

UNION FRIENDLY INN, under the auspices of the Y. M. C. A., is on Mill Street, opposite postoffice. Here can be found a temperance resort, a free reading room, supplied with all the leading periodicals of the day, a place to write letters, and a place to talk business. The room is free to every one and all are welcome. The dining room is open every day in the week. The Y. M. C. A. room is on the second floor of this building.

COURT HOUSE is on the corner of Broadway and Church Streets. It is a large stone building two stories high, and in it are most of the county offices. The court room, clerk's office, and jury rooms, are on the second floor. The grounds upon which it stands contain about six acres, and are ornamented with forest trees and laid in walks and grass plats. Religious meetings are held in this grove Sunday afternoons during the summer months.

The SUMMIT COUNTY JAIL is opposite the court house on Broadway.

CENTRAL STATION, AKRON FIRE DEPARTMENT, is on the northwest corner of High and Church Streets, immediately in the rear of the First M. E. Church. This is a fine

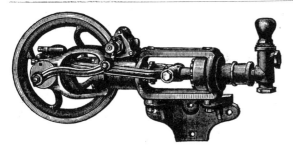
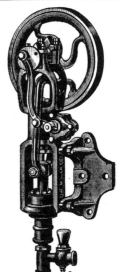

"TORRENT"

Light Power

STEAM PUMP!

Can be used horizontal or upright. Will supply 5 to 25 horse power boiler. Will pump hot or cold water. Suitable for Elevators, Stationaries, Threshing, Traction, Sawing, and a.1 other engines of less than 25 horse power.

EVERY PUMP GUARANTEED.

——Manufactured by——

THE MILLER COMPANY, CANTON, OHIO.

ESTABLISHED 1820.

Old Motto Adopted for a Certainty.

QUICK SALES and SMALL PROFITS.

We have got and will sell the best

BOOTS AND SHOES

Remember, at the Oldest Boot and Shoe House in Ohio.

J. C. BOCKIUS' SONS,

No. 8 MARKET SQUARE, CANTON, OHIO.

brick structure, and contains all the fire apparatus of the city. Part of the second floor is occupied by the City Council Chamber. The city is well supplied with a paid Fire Department, consisting of six stationary men and thirty minute men. The department has three fine steamers, one hook and ladder truck, three hose carts, and six horses. There are eighteen large supply cisterns, located in different parts of the city; a telegraph fire alarm, with thirty-six signal boxes and twenty-five miles of wire, connecting the central station with all parts of the city. Everything is of the latest and improved style, and all the apparatus' are drawn by horses.

POST OFFICE is in Masonic Temple, corner of Howard and Mill Streets.

ACADEMY OF MUSIC is on the corner of East Market and Main Streets. We give a very good illustration of this building on page 66. This edifice has a brown stone front and mansard roof, and originally cast $127,000. On the 18th of June, 1878, it was damaged by fire to the amount of about $25,000, the roof and second story being destroyed. It was immediately thereafter remodeled, and finished in April, 1879. Some important improvements were made in the building, and it is now one of the finest public audience-rooms in the country. The hall is furnished with patent opera chairs, and has a seating capacity of 1,000. It is heated by steam and lighted with gas. Three Bell telephones are in different parts of the building, connecting direct with the Fire Department. It is also provided with large water tanks and convenient hose to use in case of fire. The stage is very large, being 36x64 feet, and has all the requisite paraphernalia and modern painted scenery, comprising thirty-two complete scenes. There are five dressing-rooms and two rear entrances to the stage. Mr. J. F. Seiberling is the owner of this fine structure. Mr. W. G. Robinson is the lessee and manager of the hall.

VALLEY RAILWAY DEPOT is located at the foot of North Howard Street, and is about two squares from the business center of the city.

UNION DEPOT, of the Cleveland, Mt. Vernon & Columbus, and New York, Pennsylvania & Ohio railroads, is located just south of the corner of Mill and Prospect Streets. Last, but not least, of the prominent buildings of the city is this fine structure, and no visitor to the city should think of leaving without once seeing this grand depot. The two roads approach the depot side by side, but about one mile east of the depot they separate; the N. Y., P. & O., going east, and the C., Mt. V. & C. Road, going north. These roads cross the VALLEY RAILWAY at the Old Forge.

EAST AKRON.

What is now the Sixth Ward of Akron, was laid out in the year 1818, and called Middlebury. For a while it seemed destined to become one of the leading villages of the Western Reserve. Akron was not founded till seven years afterward. The village of Middlebury grew rapidly, and in October, 1825, a newspaper made its appearance called *The Portage Journal*. The business was so great at that time, that there were no less than sixteen stores and several mills and factories in operation. After Akron got a good start, Middlebury began to fall behind in population and interest. Akron got a start and grew rapidly, and was spreading out every year till it reached the village of Middlebury, which name it kept till about six years ago, when it was taken in as the Sixth Ward of Akron. In this ward the great sewer-pipe and stoneware works of the State are located, and has proven a valuable addition to the city. The VALLEY RAILWAY has termed this station East Akron. Their depot is a little east of Market Street, which is the longest street in the city, being about three miles long, running straight through the city from end to end. On this street are some of the finest residences in the city with the beautiful green lawns in front of them. It would pay a visitor to get off the cars at this depot and walk or ride through this street to the other part of the city, which is only one and one-half miles. You would then see the handsome part of the great city of Akron that is so well known all over the country.

BUCHTEL COLLEGE, AKRON.

BUCHTEL COLLEGE.

' This prominent and highly successful institution, named in honor of John R. Buchtel, its principal promoter and benefactor, is beautifully located in the city of Akron on an eminence said to be the highest point of land in the State of Ohio. The view from this site is a magnificent one, commanding a panoramic environment of scenery embracing the busy and wide-spreading city, with its handsome churches, prosperous manufactories, elegant residences and tree-embowered thoroughfares and fine fertile undulating country for many miles around. It is, indeed, a charming spot, and its selection as the site of the imposing edifice that crowns it so nobly, is indicative of excellent judgment on the part of the large hearted projectors and founders of this grand institution of learning.

This college was founded, is owned and controlled, by the Ohio Convention of Universalists; but it is largely an Akron institution, having been projected, and in the main endowed, by her citizens. It took its name from Hon. John R. Buchtel, who has been its most generous benefactor, and who has consecrated his life, energy and wealth, to its support. Not only in its brightest day of honor and prosperity has he stood ready to promote it, but in its darkest hours of trial and financial embarrassment, he has boldly stepped forward and raised it above danger.

In addition to his first subscription of $31,000, he has from time to time made new gifts until they have reached the magnificent aggregate of $75,000; and in further addition he has recently pledged available real estate (mostly in the city of Akron) valued at $35,000. This last liberal pledge is for the purpose of perpetual endowment, and is given on condition that the entire debt of the college be raised on or before July 1st, 1881. This debt, which on February 1st, 1879, was $61,517.12, has since that time been reduced by subscriptions to about $16,700, and the canvass still progresses favorably, there being no doubt whatever that the debt will be raised before the limit of time is reached. Mr. Buchtel is a plain, unostentatious man; but he is blessed with a largeness of the heart and nobleness of purpose, that few have the fortune to possess.

Besides the endowments of Mr. Buchtel, there are four Professorships endowed as follows: The Messenger Professorships of Mental and Moral Philosophy, of $25,000, endowed by Mrs. L. A. E. Messenger, of Akron; the Hilton Professorship of Modern Languages, endowed by John H. Hilton, of Akron; the Pierce Professorships of Natural Science, of $25,000, named in honor of Mrs. Chloe Pierce, of Sharpsville, Pa., who contributed $10,000, the remaining $10,000 being raised under the auspices of the Woman's Centenary Association, and the Buchtel Professorship of English Literature, of $20,000, endowed by Mrs. Elizabeth Buchtel, wife of John R. Buchtel, of Akron, Ohio. The college is also endowed by thirty Perpetual Scholarships of $1,000 each.

This college is open alike to students of both sexes, and all are admitted to equal privileges and by showing equal worth may attain equal honors. Although it is conducted under the auspices of a religious denomination, no restrictions are imposed upon students in the full exercise of religious opinions of whatever phase, and in its management it is in no sense sectarian. While *all* religious opinions are *respected, none are taught.*

OFFICERS OF THE BOARD.

John R. Buchtel, President; Albert B. Tinker, Secretary; Joy H. Pendleton, Treasurer.

Executive Committee—J. R. Buchtel, A. B. Tinker, J. H. Pendleton, E. P. Green, J. T. Trowbridge.

Committee on Teachers—A. C. Voris, S. M. Burnham, N. D. Tibbals.

OFFICERS OF INSTRUCTION.

Rev. Orello Cone, D. D., President, Professor of Mental and Moral Sciences; E. Fraunfelter, A. M. Ph. D., Professor of Mathematics; Charles M. Knight, A. M., Professor of Natural Science; Carl F. Kolbe, A. M., Professor of Modern Languages; Benj. T. Jones, A. M., Professor of Ancient Languages; Maria Parsons, Professor of Rhetoric and English Literature; Jennie Gifford, B. S., Professor of Normal Department and Principal of Preparatory School; W. D. Shipman, A. M., Adjunct Professor of Ancient Languages; James H. Aydelott, B. S., Adjunct Professor of Mathematics; Arthur S. Kimball, Teacher of Voice Culture and Harmony; Ella H. Morrison, Teacher of Instrumental Music.

The College Cerriculum now comprises three distinct courses—clasical, scientific, and philosophical—each of four years, with a three years' preparatory course for each college course. These are equal to the best standards adopted by the leading institutions of the country.

The expenses are as reasonable as those of any similar institution of the country.

For information, address the Secretary, A. B. Tinker.

SPRINGFIELD.

As there is no village within several miles of the VALLEY RAILWAY depot, we will give a short history of the township. A postoffice has lately been established near the depot under the name of Krumroy postoffice; thus the name of the station has been changed from Springfield to Krumroy.

The township stands number one in mineral and agricultural products. It has a rich, black, sandy loam soil, and a hardy, industrious population, largely of German descent, which has given much of it the appearance of a garden. Stone coal is abundant, but the great mineral wealth of the township consists in the potter's clay, fire-proof brick clay, and sewer-pipe clay. This township furnishes the clay from which three millions, three hundred and fifty thousand eight hundred gallons of pottery ware is annually manufactured in Summit County alone. Large quantities are taken to Canada and manufactured there, to save the tariff duty on manufactured articles.

SLOSS BRO'S BLOCK, COR. SUPERIOR AND SENECA STS., CLEVELAND.—(See page 15.)

The center of the township is covered by a beautiful lake, called Springfield Lake, of about a mile in diameter. This lake is about four miles east of the VALLEY RAILWAY depot.

There are three thriving and pleasant villages in the township—North Springfield, Mogadore and Millheim. A number of potteries are situated near this village. The first settler in the township was Ariel Bradley, who came into the township in 1808 and settled near where Mogadore has since been located. Here he built the first house in the township. As the Little Cuyahoga River runs through the township, it furnishes some fine mill-sites. One branch of it rises in Suffield Lake, the other in Springfield Lake. To secure a full supply of water at all times, a company of mill owners, several years ago, got an act of Legislature authorizing them to raise Springfield Lake six feet, and lower it four feet from its natural level. As the lake is a mile in diameter, this rise and fall affords, in dry weather, a supply of water for the Akron mills when other sources fail.

RESTAURANT.

Opposite Valley Depot, GREENTOWN, OHIO.

Groceries, Choice Wines, Fresh Lager, Cigars, &c

Always on hand. Meals served up in best of style at all hours.

WM. F. HAAK, Proprietor.

LAKE FLOURING MILLS, GREENTOWN, O.,

DELANY & BALL, Proprietors.

Do Custom and Merchant Work. Flour and Feed Always on hand.

SHANAFELT & SHAFER,
——Dealers in——

Dry Goods, Boots and Shoes, Notions,

GLASSWARE, QUEENSWARE, HARDWARE, &C.,

GREENTOWN, O.

JACOB HISSNER, Greentown, Ohio,

Dealer in First-class Draft and Driving Horses

BUYING AND SELLING ALL THE TIME.

GREENTOWN HOTEL,

JOHN GREENWALD, Proprietor.

A Livery is conducted in connection with the Hotel.

WISE & ACKER,

Founders, Mnfs. of Plows, Wheel Cultivators, Scrapers, and other Castings

GREENTOWN, OHIO.

HENRY SHANAFELT & SON,

Dealers in Groceries and Provisions, and Raw Furs,

Also, Nursery Stock, Small Fruits, &c.,

GREENTOWN, OHIO.

11

BARBER MATCH FACTORY, AKRON.

The opposite cut represents all the buildings of the BARBER MATCH CO., which are divided into rooms as follows:

4 rooms	85x36 each	12;240 square feet of Flooring.
3 ,,	65x36 ,,	7,020 ,, ,, ,,
3 ,,	87x38 ,,	9,918 ,, ,, ,,
3 ,,	85x45 ,,	11,475 ,, ,, ,,
3 ,,	75x36 ,,	8,100 ,, ,, ,,
3 ,,	100x45 ,,	13,500 ,, ,, ,,
4 ,,	50x45 ,,	9,000 ,, ,, ,,
2 ,,	50x32 ,,	3,200 ,, ,, ,,
1 ,,	172x45 ,,	7,740 ,, ,, ,,
1 ,,	60x40 ,,	2,400 ,, ,, ,,
1 ,,	60x50 ,,	3,000 ,, ,, ,,
4 ,,	75x35 ,,	10,500 ,, ,, ,,
4 ,,	65x35 ,,	9,100 ,, ,, ,,
2 ,,	42x18 ,,	1,512 ,, ,, ,,
2 ,,	60x36 ,,	4,320 ,, ,, ,,
4 Fire Proof Vaults	40x10 ,,	1,600 ,, ,, ,,
Total		114,625 ,, ,, ,,

or equal to one room 22 feet in width by over one mile in length. These works are the result of over 33 years' experience, the business having been established by Geo. Barber in the year 1847. It has the most complete Match Machinery in the world, run by a 275 horse power engine, the possible production being over 90,000,000 matches per day of 24 hours. The buildings ar · heated by steam, ventilated by exhaust fans, and lighted by electric lights. To itemize the materials used in these works yearly, would be entering into details unnecessarily, but if the possible production of this company were placed end to end they would complete the circuit of the earth every seven days. This company pays one-sixth of the Internal Revenue derived from matches, and if run to the full capacity would pay yearly as much as any three factories in the country. They make a greater variety of matches, and more attractive styles of packages than all the other factories of the country combined; and are so protected by patents on both machinery and matches as to challenge the competition of the world. Their goods are sold by all reliable wholesale and retail dealers at prices as low as any in the market. Call for the Diamond Cut Stick, with two thin edges and a heavy center, which makes it kindle quick and gives it a strong blaze, thus combining all the advantages of a thin and heavy stick,

BARBER MATCH CO.,
SOLE MANUFACTURERS,
AKRON, OHIO.

This circumstance, illustrating early life in this township, is worth preserving. In the same year with Bradley, John Hail and his younger brother, both of them under eighteen years of age, came into the township and settled on a farm on which, till several years ago, he resided. There was not a road to or from his cabin. As the Indians were plenty, and not always friendly, he and his brother dare not sleep in the house, but at night would make a fire, to give it the appearance of their being there, and then take their guns and go into a cornfield near by to sleep. In this manner they passed the first summer and fall.

UNIONTOWN.

The village of Uniontown is situated in Lake Township, Stark County, forty-five miles south of Cleveland on the line of the VALLEY RAILWAY. Part of the following is taken from a history of the village written by a lady some time ago, but has never been published. The village is situated in a healthy and fertile part of the country. It contains at present about three hundred inhabitants who are intelligent and enterprising, and are making rapid advancements in the various branches of the sciences, agriculture and arts. Uniontown was laid out in the year 1816, by Thomas Albert, assisted by a Mr Banner and G. Myers. At this time only one dwelling house was to be seen in the place where the village now stands, and here the father of Mr. Albert resided. But several families lived in the vicinity, and all seemed to take a lively interest in the welfare and prosperity of the new village. They desired it to be called Albertsville, in honor of its founder, but he declined the honor. The appellation of Uniontown was determined to be conferred upon it. The first house erected was built by Mr. Albert, which is still standing and is at present occupied. About the same time great numbers of people were emigrating from the eastern States—chiefly from Pennsylvania—to this part of the country, who immediately commenced putting up buildings, and Uniontown for a while appeared to be in a flourishing condition. A small log house was put up in 1817, on the same square which is now used as a church yard. Here the first school was taught by a young man named Alexander Constant, who was of German descent. The next year a school was opened for the teaching of both German and English. The first sermon was preached in the school house, even before it was finished, by Rev. Fouse, in 1817. The corner stone of the Lutheran and Reformed Church was laid in the spring of 1830, and the following year it was dedicated. Rev. Fouse continued as pastor of this church until his death, which occurred three years later. The first death occurred in the year 1831, that of a child, a daughter of Mr. Gottshall, and this was the first person buried in the now densely crowded churchyard. The first marriage in the village took place in 1819, between Richard Rhodes and Catherine Haynes. In 1825 Jos. T. Holloway was appointed the first postmaster and since then there has been but six postmasters in Uniontown. The first physician was a man named Lyncoln, but he made only a temporary stay, and in 1823 another by the name of Devoe arrived, and remained until his death, which occurred several years later. The first tavern was kept by Mr. Stadden in the year 1822, and about the same time a small store was opened by Myers & Gieswite. This was the first mercantile business transacted in the village of Uniontown. From the year 1824 to 1830, Uniontown appeared to be in a backward state, and it was even apprehended that it would not revive. But about this time there were many new arrivals, and it again began to prosper. In 1840 a great political excitement prevailed in Stark County, and particularly at Uniontown. Many an able oration was delivered, and political questions discussed in the grove north of the village by eminent men from surrounding villages and counties. Ever since it has continued to improve, and is now a thriving village. At present Uniontown has three churches, a Methodist, Lutheran and

OGDEN HOUSE, CANTON, O.

H KERSHAW ENG

THE FINEST AND ONLY FIRST-CLASS HOTEL BUILDING IN THE CITY
LARGE AND COMMODIOUS ROOMS,

And Convenient to the Business part of the City.   The ceilings of the rooms are all high
which makes them THE COOLEST AND MOST COMFORTABLE rooms in the City.

MOST CONVENIENT TO THE RAILROADS.

W. M. SHORB, Proprietor.

BOOKS, STATIONERY, &C., &C., &C.

WM. B. PERKINS & CO.,

THE LEADING

Booksellers, Stationers and Wall Paper Dealers

OF STARK COUNTY.

OPPOSITE ST. CLOUD HOTEL, CANTON, OHIO.

All the Best Books received as soon as Published.

OFFICE AND FINE STATIONERY A SPECIALTY.

Sole Agents for Thomas' Ink, Sheet's Writing Fluids, Champion Copying Inks, best in
use.   Blank Books, all kinds and made to order.

PRINTING DONE AT SHORT NOTICE AND LOW PRICES.

Agents of the American Book Exchange.   Mail Orders receive prompt attention.

Reformed. One flour mill, seven stores, two blacksmith shops, two carriage shops, and a hotel. The village is one mile east of the VALLEY RAILWAY depot, but a hack runs to and from all trains.*

GREENTOWN.

The village of Greentown is situated in Lake Township, Stark County, and is forty-eight and one-half miles south of Cleveland and ten miles north of Canton on the line of the VALLEY RAILWAY. The depot is three-fourths of a mile west of the place. The vilage was laid out about the year 1812 by Peter Dickerhoof and Henry Wise, who at the time owned adjoining quarter sections of land, the town being one half on each quarter. It will be seen from the above date, that Greentown is old enough to be a city, but it has never had the requisite population. The first house built in the place was a story and a-half log house, by an Irishman named McNab, and was for a number of years kept by him as a hotel. For many years the business of the place was in the hands of the village store-keeper, blacksmith, cooper, etc. About the year 1838, William Ball, and his four sons, John, Ephriam, William and Adin, started a foundry here. For some time they were chiefly engaged in the manufacture of stoves and plows. In the course of a few years, on account of some financial embarrassments, other men—Michael Wise, Jacob H. Wise, and Lewis Acker, having means, were induced to go into the firm, when the Balls, except Ephriam, retired from it. The new firm, in addition to the former business, engaged in building the "Hussey Reaper," and "Pitts' Separator." In the spring of 1850, Cornelius Aultman and Lewis Miller bought the interests of the Wise's and Acker's. The firm name then became Ball, Aultman & Co. About this time the Pittsburgh, Fort Wayne & Chicago Railroad was built through Canton, and this enterprising firm removed to that place, and the little Greentown Foundry and Machine Shops developed into the mammoth concern now known as the Buckeye Works, which now have shops both in Canton and Akron. What was Greentown's loss was Canton's gain, for to that establishment is largely due Canton's growth and prosperity in the last thirty years. A few years later another foundry was started by Henry Shanafelt and Christian Kryder. They too, engaged in the stove and plow manufacture. This shop is still in operation. It was run for a number of years by Levi Kryder, now of Akron. The shop is now run by Wise & Acker. The village at present has a population of about three hundred. It has a hotel, one very nice M. E. Church, a good district school, which is kept in operation ten months in the year, a flour mill, foundry, and several stores.

The village is located in the midst of one of the finest agricultural districts in the State. The place is noted for its healthfulness and the longevity of its people. There are six or eight persons who have passed four-score, and a larger number that have reached the allotted time of man. The people are a very clever and enterprising class, as will be seen by the business cards on pages 77 and 81. It is worthy of note to know that this is the birthplace of Messrs. Lewis and Jacob Miller, (whose birthplace can be seen from the cars on the right soon after leaving the depot, going south. It is an old log hut on the side of the hill) C. Aultman, and a host of others, now of Canton and Akron; in fact, for thirty years it has been a kind of recruiting port from which those two cities have drawn many of the good citizens.

The sewer-pipe works of Stripe Brothers, and the drain-tile works of Isaac Stripe, are near Greentown, on the east side of the VALLEY RAILWAY. The coal bank of Smith,

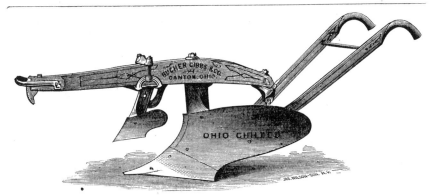
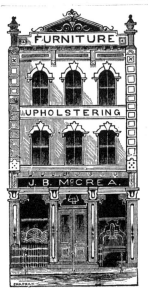

Borst & Co., is situated near the depot, on the east side of the track.   Coal of a very good quality is taken from this bank in large quantities and shipped over the VALLEY RAIL-WAY.

A few rods north of the depot, on the east side, is a beautiful little grove owned by J. A. Borst, termed Water Shed Park.   (See engraving below.)   The whole tract of bottom land north was formerly called the "wild meadow," and considered worthless land.   It was swampy, and most of it was covered with a thick growth of underbrush.   Cattle were turned loose on this meadow, and in many instances they would sink deep into the mire and die.   This tract was, a few years ago, purchased by Mr. Borst, drained and cleared, and is now becoming very fine farming land.   Some fine crops have been raised upon it this season.   The park is situated on the highest ridge of the State, whence the waters divide, part going to Lake Erie, and part to the Gulf of Mexico.   The elevation at this

WATER SHED PARK, GREENTOWN.

point is 555 feet above Lake Erie.   The waters can be seen to divide in the grove.   It has been fitted up with accommodations for small picnics, there being a spring of clear, sparkling water in the grove.

NEW BERLIN.

The village of New Berlin is situated in Plain Township, Stark County, and on the line of the VALLEY RAILWAY.   It is very pleasantly located on high ground, thus com-manding a view of the surrounding country for some distance.   The place was settled in the year 1826, and has been gaining ever since, and now has a population of about four hundred, most of which are Germans.   It has a good school, three churches, two dry-goods stores, three groceries, a tavern, blacksmith and cabinet shops, lumber yards, etc., thus making a very thriving and growing place, and the people look forward to the time when it will be classed as a city.   The VALLEY RAILWAY station is about one and one-fourth miles west of the village.

12

CITY OF CANTON.

Canton, the county seat of Stark County, is finely situated in the forks of the Nimishillen Creek, a tributary of the Muskingum. It is the southern terminus of the VALLEY RAILWAY, fifty-nine miles south of Cleveland, and on the line of the Pittsburgh, Fort Wayne & Chicago Railroad, 102 miles from Pittsburgh, and 366 miles from Chicago. It was laid out by Bezaleel Wells, of Steubenville, in 1806, three years before the organization of Stark County. The original plat, as recorded in the clerk's office in Columbiana County, to which the territory then belonged, was bounded on the north by North Street, on the east by East Alley, (now called Saxton Street), on the south by South street, and on the west by West Street, (now called Wells.) Subsequently there were contentions about the metes and bounds of lots when Mr. Wells, in 1823, had the plat recorded in the clerk's office in Canton, and by way of explanation, appended a note of which the following is an abstract: " Said proprietor, did further declare, that in laying out the said lots, in order to cover any inaccuracies which might be made in measurements, the chain used was a few inches longer than the exact length of a common surveyor's chain, by which it appears that there is an excess in the size of the lots when they came to be subjected to strict measurements; and lastly, the said proprietor does declare and make known, that he relinquished all claims to said excess of ground, and desires that it may be considered as the property of the present owners of said lots respectively, and such was his original intention in laying out said lots." The southwest block of lots, were donated for a "graveyard," the last block on Tuscarawas Street, south side, "for a house of worship," and the block opposite, "for an academy or public school." Neither of these lots are numbered in the original plat.

The first building in Canton was on Market Street, east side, between Fourth and Fifth. It was a log cabin, about eighteen feet square, erected in the fall of 1806, by Garret Crusen, for a tavern. It contained but one room, and had two small shed additions;

FIRST COURT HOUSE, CANTON, BUILT IN 1811.

one was used as a bed-room, and the other as a cellar and store house. The large room was appropriated for a bar, kitchen, dining and sitting-room.

The following summer, James F. Leonard, who came into the country two years previous, and was the first white settler, erected a brick house, on the southwest corner of Market and Seventh, which was the first building of that material in the country. This old building was torn down last year to give place to the present building of Sherrick & Miller.

About this time the object of a new county seat was agitated. Osnaburgh, five miles east, had previously been laid out, and had considerably the start of Canton. There were with many, serious objections to Canton, because of its location in the "Plains"—the supposed scarcity of building material and the imaginary severity of the cold winds. The rivalry of the two towns waxed warm. James Leeper, the proprietor of Osnaburgh, was a man of dissolute habits, and lacked integrity, while Wells, proprietor of Canton, had an unexceptionable reputation, and having been a member of the convention that framed the first constitution of Ohio, gave him more than an ordinary amount of influence. This circumstance, in connection with the fact that he proposed donating to the county 150 lots, influenced the commissioners to locate the county seat

—THE—

GREAT BUCKEYE MANUFACTORY,

C. Aultman & Co, Canton, O.

The above sketch suggests the remarkably effective threshing machinery as now constructed by the great house of C. AULTMAN & CO. The threshers made at this factory have a world-wide renown; and with each of these machines is now furnished, when desired, an engine which besides being adapted to every form of operation requiring power, is also a safe and complete road locomotive. The demand for these equipments is enormous, taxing to the utmost the works of C. Aultman & Co. notwithstanding their immense capacity, some idea of which can be formed from the following extract, which we take from a late number of the Chicago *Illustrated World:*

This colossal establishment took its start in Canton in the year 1851, with a working capital not exceeding $4,500. The original proprietors were Cornelius Aultman, Lewis Miller, Jacob Miller, and Geo. Cook, the latter now deceased. They and their associates were the original inventors and patentees of all the Buckeye harvesting machines. The more recent additions to their list of successful manufactures are the "Buckeye Self-binding Harvester," the "Canton Monitor Engine," and the "Traction Road Engine," all of which are well calculated to conserve the exalted reputation of this house for producing the most celebrated and efficient agricultural machines in the world. This establishment had an humble inception, but it steadily grew in extent and importance until it has become the largest and most complete manufactory of its kind in the world. The works embrace the following named structures: Building for threshing and wood-working machinery, brick, 400 by 50 feet, four floors. Reaper warehouse, brick, 181 by 60 feet, four floors. Iron machinery building, brick 147 by 60 feet, four floors. Iron finishing building, brick, 70 by 60 feet, three floors. Core, pattern and engine house, brick, 150 by 60 feet, two floors. Engine shop, brick, 302 by 50 feet, two floors. Moulding room, brick, 125 by 75 feet, one floor. Blacksmith shop and iron room, brick, 313 by 41 feet, one floor. Five acres of wooden structures, comprising wagon shop, boiler works, testing house, paint shops, store rooms for thresher and engines, etc. These structures have a total floor area of 459,528 square feet, or upwards of ten and a half acres, being some three and a half acres larger than the next largest agricultural implement works in existence. This mammoth establishment has eleven distinct departments giving employment to an aggregate of 650 skilled workmen; the monthly pay-roll amounting to $35,000. The motive power comprises two engines, each of 120 horse power, and one engine of 50 horse power. Their products find a ready and expanding market in both hemispheres. While at the works we noticed a shipment of their world-celebrated machines to Algiers, Africa. They have branch offices and supply depots at Paris, France; London, England; Baltimore, Chicago, Cincinnati and other leading distributing points, while they also have general and local agents in all the agricultural sections. Their aggregate manufactures for 1879 reached $2,000,000.

at Canton. From the sale of these lots, the county realized about $5,000. The first settlers were from Pennsylvania, Virginia and Maryland.

The first store was erected in 1807, by Abraham Kroft, in a small building, corner of Market and Fifth Streets. The goods were kept in a back room, and customers had to pass through the front room, which was used in common, as a kitcken, dining and bed-room, The stock was wagoned from Pittsburgh, and comprised only such articles as would be likely needed in a new country. John Shorb started the second store the same year, in the brick house built by Mr. Leonard. The next spring Mr. Shorb, removed his store to a building he had erected on the lot now occupied by Eagle block. The prices of staple articles at that time were as follows: Salt $3 to $4 per bushel, nails 25 cents per pound, window glass 8x10, 12½ cents per light, coffee 50 cents per pound, iron 20 cents, sole leather 50 cents a pound.

There were Indians about at that time, whose lodges were west of the Tuscarawas River. They made frequent visits among our early settlers, but were entirely harmless in their intercourse. On the breaking out of the war in 1812, they moved their quarters to Sandusky.

PRESENT COURT HOUSE, CANTON.

A postoffice was established in 1808, and Samuel Coulter was appointed postmaster. The only mail received, was from the east, on horseback, once a week. After the organization of the county, court was held at the Eagle Tavern, (now Eagle block,) kept by Philip Dewalt. Next at the tavern of Samuel Coulter, corner Market and Seventh Streets. The cellar was used as a jail. From this place it was removed to Patten's tavern, St. Cloud lot, and here continued until the completion of a double log structure, on the northeast corner of Third and Market, erected especially for a court house and jail. The north half was used as a jail and divided into two cells for the confinement of prisoners. It was constructed of a a double tier of hewed logs pinned together and weather boarded on the sonth half, which was used as a court room, until a brick court house was built on the square in 1816. The log structure was retained as a jail until the erection of the new edifice in 1831. The present court house is a fine structure, and an honor to the city. It is built of brick and ornamented with stone. It was erected in the year 1870, on the ground formerly occupied by the old brick court house, which was erected in 1866, on the northwest corner of public square. There are two domes upon the present building, one of which has the town clock upon it. On the grounds on the south side of the building is a large and beautiful fountain. Immediately in the rear of the court house is the county jail. We give an exact representation of the old and present court houses on pages 90 and 92.

The first number of the *The Ohio Repository* was published in Canton, in March, 1815, by John Saxton, who remained at the head of that paper until November, 1868, when the *Repository* and *Republican* were consolidated, Mr. Saxton continuing as one of its editors up to the time of his death, which occurred in April, 1871, he being at that time the oldest editor (connected with one paper) in the United States. The *Republican* had been published for ten years by Josiah Hartzell. The present *Canton Repository*, under the control of Thomas W. Saxton & Co., is a journal of extensive circulation, and wields a large influence.

In 1834, a canal was projected from Canton to Sandyville, connecting at that place with the Sandy and Beaver Canal, which terminated at Bolivar. It was chartered under the name of "Nimishillen & Sandy Slack Water Navigation Company," and was regarded at the time, a great enterprise, affording as it would, water communications with Pittsburgh and Cleveland. Real estate, especially water lots, changed hands at exorbitant prices. The canal commenced at the north end of Walnut Street, which was excavated through its whole length, and down to the south creek, where the slack water part commenced. The head feeder was to be the middle of the branch of the Nimishillen, tapped near Reed's bridge. The year following, a financial crisis overran the country, and work on the Sandy and Beaver was suspended. Stockholders of the "side

cut" began to lose confidence in the enterprise, and refused to pay up installments due; as a consequence, further progress ceased and was not again resumed. All traces of the canal are now obliterated.

The first addition to the original plat of Canton was made by Henry Slusser in 1836. The next was in 1851 by Frederick Young, H. H. Myers, and D. Raffensperger. Since that time there have been ninety-one new additions accepted by the city council, sixty of which were in the last ten years. The population of the place in 1840, was 2,136; in 1850, 2,740; in 1860, 4,442. The census of 1880 gives it a population of 12,258.

EAGLE BLOCK, COR. TUSCARAWAS AND MARKET STS., CANTON.

The city is supplied with water from the West Nimishillen Creek, the water works being located a little north of the VALLEY RAILWAY crossing on West Tuscarawas Street. The water is unfit for drinking purposes, but comes very handy to wash pavements and sprinkle lawns; and in case of fires, the fire hydrants placed at the principal street crossings are brought into active service and do effective work.

At present Canton has three railroads—the Pittsburgh, Fort Wayne & Chicago, passing through from east to west; the VALLEY RAILWAY, coming in from the north, and the little narrow gauge Connotton Valley, coming up from the coal fields in the south. With all these, and the various manufactories, Canton has before her a brilliant future, and is destined to grow still more rapidly in commercial and industrial importance and wealth.

PUBLIC PARKS AND CEMETERIES.

The city of Canton is unfortunate in not having any parks or public places of resort. There is no public park or grove near the city where the weary visitor could find a seat, or the hard working mechanic a resting place. The only place of any account near Canton is Myer's Lake, and that is about three miles from the city. This is a pleasant spot, but of no account to the city of Canton in the way of supplying the place of a public park.

The PUBLIC CEMETERY of Canton is at the west end of Tuscarawas Street. It contains some very handsome and costly monuments, and many old and curious tombstones, some of which have very curious and amusing epitaphs upon them. In passing through this cemetery and reading the various epitaphs, reminds a person of the old English graveyards, where they put almost anything on a tombstone that would make a rhyme.

A Beautiful Summer Resort.

High Bridge Glens & Caves

CUYAHOGA FALLS, Ohio.

The town of Cuyahoga Falls has of late become quite noted as a summer resort, and is annually visited by thousands of pleasure-seekers. It is in summit County, on the beautiful river Cuyahoga, and derives its name from the numerous falls and cascades in the river at this point. It is thirty-six miles south of Cleveland, and four miles from Akron, the county seat, and is accessible by four daily express trains on the Cleveland, Mount Vernon & Columbus Railroad.

One-fourth of a mile from the centre of the town is a bridge which spans a narrow gorge in the river, one hundred feet above its bed. At this point, the entrance to the glens and caves, a rude stairway has been constructed, which leads down to a plateau, where has been erected a building with a spacious dining-room and kitchen attached, where dinner and other parties are served refreshments, and under the same roof is a restaurant, where everything in the line of refreshments can be had. On this level is also a fine croquet ground, and numerous rustic seats, shadowed by overhanging, high perpendicular rocks.

A few feet below is *Lovers' Retreat*, a broad ledge of rocks, shadowed by large forest trees; and down still another flight of stairs, close by the river side, hedged in by rustic work, is a broad, level surface, which forms the entrance to *Fern Cave*, a subterranean cavity in the solid rock, 35x54 feet in dimensions. This retreat is supplied with numerous rude seats of iron and wood, where those weary from climbing can rest. Leaving the cave, we pass down the strongly braced stairway, running diagonally with the face of the wall, and reach *Observation Rock*, a huge stone of over one hundred tons weight. From this point a magnificent view is presented to the eye. Looking back and up the stream, one gets a fine view of the water falls above, or from fifteen to twenty feet in height; also High Bridge, some eighty feet above. Still farther below, and immediately under *Fern Cave*, is *Doves' Retreat*, a huge cavern, with an overhanging roof of rock twenty-five feet above. To the right and down the stream is *Suspension Bridge*, which crosses the stream above high-water mark. It is made of strong rods of iron, crossing the chasm, securely fastened to huge boulders upon either side, with strong hand-rails, and affords a secure passage over the foaming, surging waters below. Crossing the bridge, we are upon the east side of the river, near *Cascade Point*, which is a lovely retreat, reached by a path made of rocks and boulders, under *Weeping Cliffs*, a solid wall of overhanging rock, one hundred feet in height, and fringed at the top with hemlock and birch trees. Here a beautiful spring of cold mineral water gushes forth from the face of the rock, climbing over and around a high point. A broad avenue is presented, which borders the rugged bed of the stream for a mile. This is called the *Grand Promenade*, and is hedged in on one side by lofty, overhanding rocks, and on the other by innumerable shade trees and the winding river. Here sunlight has to struggle for an entrance, and it is always a cool and romantic retreat. Swings and croquet here abound. Ferns and mosses literally cover the grounds and rocks upon every side.

The proprietors have recently been to great expense in improving this delightful retreat, and are every day adding to the numerous attractions, with a view of making this, as it is fast becoming, the most *popular* resort in Ohio. It is already the most *attractive*.

Special arrangements can be made by large parties wishing to visit the resort, on application by letter. Sabbath School and Society excursions solicited. A fact worthy of note is, that all trains stop within five rods of the entrance to the grounds. For further particulars, address

HIGH BRIDGE GLEN CO.

The Old Cemetery is on South Plum Street, corner Tenth Street. Reform Cemetery, East Tuscarawas Street; Rowland Cemetery, East Tuscarawas Street, east of city limits; Lutheran Cemetery, corner East Tuscarawas and Herbruck Streets.

CHURCHES.

Canton has a number of very fine church edifices, several of which cost $50,000 each. We give below the location of all churches in the city, which are fourteen in number:

PALMERS'S; S. MARKET ST., CANTON. (Page 45.)

First Baptist Church, southwest corner of Market and Ninth Streets.

Church of Christ, corner of Poplar and Seventh Streets.

Friedens Evangelical Church, (German and English), southeast corner Fourth and Herbruck Streets.

St. Paul's Episcopal Church, corner Poplar and Tenth Streets.

English Lutheran Church, north side of West Tuscarawas, between Poplar and Plum Streets.

First M. E. Church, southwest corner Tuscarawas and Poplar Streets.

Second M. E. Church, South Market Street

First Presbyterian Church, southwest corner Tuscarawas and Plum Streets.

Reformed Jerusalem Church (German Congregation) East Tuscarawas, west of Herbruck Street.

Trinity Church, (Sscond Reform) East Tuscarawas Street.

Evangelical Lutheran Church, corner East Tuscarawas and Herbruck Streets.

United Brethren in Christ Church, corner Charles and Willett Streets.

St. John's Catholic Church, (English) northwest corner Plum and North Streets.

St. Peter's Catholic Church, (German) southeast corner Poplar and Louis Avenue.

SCHOOLS.

The people of Canton take great pride in their public schools, and they have abundant reasons for so doing. The buildings are large and fitted up for the health and comfort of the scholars. They are ably conducted and will compare favorably with any in the country. The location of the principal school buildings are as follows: North School, corner of North Cherry Street and Lawrence Avenue; South School, east side of Market Street, south of the P., Ft. W. & C. Railroads; East School, corner of Fifth and Herbruck Streets; West School, northwest corner of West Tuscarawas and Plum Streets. In addition to the public schools, there are several select and Catholic schools in the city.

VARIOUS INSTITUTIONS AND BUILDINGS.

Canton is well protected against fires. It has one steamer and eight hose companies located in different parts of the city. The central engine house is on the southeast corner of Poplar and Eighth Streets. The POSTOFFICE is on the southwest corner of South Market and Eighth Streets.

The COUNTY INFIRMARY, for the support of the indigent, is situated on a farm about one mile from Canton. The farm is under a high state of cultivation, and the Infirmary is under most excellent direction, and is one of the best in the State.

EAGLE BLOCK, the finest block in the city, is a brick structure four stories high, on the corner of Tuscarawas and Market Streets, opposite the court house.

VIEW IN THE HIGH BRIDGE GLENS.—(See page 95.)

BIOGRAPHICAL

JEPTHA H. WADE,

President of the Valley Railway Company.

Jeptha H. Wade, whose name has been prominently connected with the telegraph history of the west, and associated with many other important enterprises, was born in Seneca Co., N. Y., in 1811. He is a son of Jeptha Wade, a surveyor and civil engineer, and was brought up to mechanical pursuits, in which he achieved a fair amount of success.

In 1844 news came to him of the excitement created by the success of the experiment of working a telegraph line between Baltimore and Washington. He turned his attention to the new science, studied it with his accustomed patience and assiduity, mastered its details so far as then understood, and immediately saw the advantage to the country, and the pecuniary benefit to those immediately interested, likely to accrue from the extension of the telegraph system which had just been created.

He entered earnestly on the work of extending this system, and the first line west of Buffalo was built by him on the M. C. R. R. The Jackson office was opened and operated by him, although he had received no practical instruction in the manipulation of the instruments. After a short interval, he again entered the field of construction, and, working with untiring energy, soon covered Ohio and the country as far west as St. Louis, with a net-work of wires known as the "Wade lines."

This was not accomplished, however, without experiencing the difficulties, annoyances and misfortunes, to which all great enterprises are subject in their infancy. Ignorant employees, imperfect insulation, and ruinous competition, were the greatest embarrassments. But to Mr. Wade, these obstacles were not unsurmountable, and in the face of all these difficulties, he proceeded with the work of opening and operating telegraph lines. Imperfect insulation was met by the invention of the famous "Wade insulator," which is still in use.

He was the first to enclose a submarine cable, in iron armor, across the Mississippi River at St. Louis, for which invention the world and its telegraph system owes him much; as it was this important discovery and improvement in their construction, that made telegraph cables a success, and the crossing of oceans a possibility.

The "House consolidation" placed his interests in the Erie & Michigan, and Wade lines in the hands of the Mississippi Valley Printing Telegraph Co. This consolidation was followed by the union of all the House and Morse lines in the west and the organization of the Western Union Telegraph Co. In all these acts of consolidation, the influence of Mr. Wade was active and powerful. Realizing the fact that competition between short lines rendered them unproductive, and that in telegraphy, as in other things, union is strength, he directed his energies to bringing about the consolidation; not only of the lines connecting with each other, but of rival interests. The soundness of his judgment has been proven, by the remarkable prosperity of the lines since their consolidation in marked contrast with their former condition. He was one of the originators of the first Pacific telegraph, and on the formation of the Company, was made its President.

The location of the line, and its construction through the immense territory, then in great part a wilderness between Chicago and San Francisco, were now left mainly to his unaided judgment; and here again those qualities converted a hazardous experiment into a brilliant success. He remained President of the Pacific Company until he secured its consolidation with the Western Union Telegraph Company, to accomplish which he went to California in the latter part of 1860, and succeeded in harmonizing the jarring telegraphic institutions there. On the completion of this arrangement, in 1866, Mr. Wade was made President of the consolidated Company, having his headquarters in New York. It is scarcely possible to over-estimate the value of his connection with the Western Union Telegraph Company at this period of its history, especially after he became its chief executive officer. He possessed, in a superior degree, the invaluable faculty of administration, and the power of clear, accurate, discriminating systemization.

The telegraph had brought to Mr. Wade vast wealth, but it had also brought him into a state of health which imperiled its enjoyment. To dismiss care he sold out his telegraph interests, and gave himself up to needed rest and recuperation. On his restoration of health, which followed a judicious respite from labor, he entered into many spheres of active life. The wealth he has accumulated is mostly invested in such a manner as to largely aid in building up the prosperity of Cleveland. The large and pleasant tract of land in the Seventeenth Ward, known as "Wade Park," was purchased and beautified at his own expense, for the enjoyment of the public. At the organization of the Citizens' Savings and Loan Association, of Cleveland, in 1867, he was elected its President, and still retains that office. He is the originator and President of the Lake View Cemetery Association. As a leading Director in many of the largest factories, banks, and public institutions, his clear head and active judgment are highly valued. He is a Director of the Second National Bank, of Cleveland; a Director of the Cleveland Rolling Mill Company, Cleveland Iron Mining Company, and Union Steel Screw Company, and the President of the American Sheet and Boiler Plate Company, and President of the Chicago & Atchison Bridge Company. He is also a Director in several railroad companies, and the President of the Kalamazoo, Allegan & Grand Rapids, and the Cincinnati, Wabash & Michigan R. R. Co.'s. He is besides President of the VALLEY RAILWAY, running from Cleveland towards the coal fields of Ohio. This will be a valuable acquisition to the interests of Cleveland, and under the management of Mr. Wade, will be promptly carried forward. The VALLEY RAILWAY was projected previous to the the panic of 1873, which put a stop to it. As the times began to improve, vigorous efforts were made to carry it forward, but met with but little success, until the summer of 1878. The importance of this Road was strongly advocated by the newspapers, meetings of the citizens were held, and a general interest awakened. Under this impetus the Road was put under contract, and considerable progress was made in the work, when it was checked by a controversy between the contractors and the company. Before this a contract had been made by the city of Cleveland with the VALLEY RAILWAY for the transfer to the company of that portion of the bed of the Ohio canal sold to the city by the state, which would give the railroad the most desirable entrance into the city, and access to shipping facilities on the lake. The terms of this contract had not been complied with, and its abrogation by the city was threatened. At this juncture the management of the VALLEY RAILWAY succeded in effecting a negotiation with capitalists for the amount necessary to complete and equip the Road, but the parties who agreed to lend the money demanded as a condition that Mr. Wade should become the President. Mr. Wade took the matter into consideration and announced his willingness to assume the position, if the canal bed negotiation could be satisfactorily adjusted. The City Council met the difficulty by a resolution authorizing the Mayor to make and sign a new contract on terms satisfactory to Mr. Wade and the VALLEY RAILWAY COMPANY. The Company was reorganized with Mr. Wade at its head; the difficulties with the contractors were satisfactorily adjusted, work was resumed, and the Road completed and regular trains commenced running from Cleveland to Canton March 1st, 1880.

In additiog to his having other manifold duties, Mr. Wade has been appointed commissioner of the City Sinking Fund, Park Commissioner, and Director of the Work House and House of Refuge. He is one of the trustees of the Cleveland Protestant Orphan Asylum, and is now building for that purpose, at his own expense, a magnificent fire-proof building sufficiently large to accommodate from one hundred to one hundred and fifty children. The building is located on St. Clair Street, and will be completed in a few months. Mr. Wade has also contributed freely to many other charitable objects. He is now in the zenith of his power, and is universally beloved by the people of the beautiful city which he has made his home, and which he has done so much to enlarge and adorn, and by the many recipents of his unostentious charities.—*History Cuyahoga County, 1880.*

SYLVESTER T. EVERETT,

Vice President and Treasurer Valley Railway.

The subject of this sketch, a son of Samuel Everett, a prominent merchant and manufacturer; was born in Liberty township, Trumbull County, Ohio, on the 27th of November, 1838. He was educated in the common schools of his native town and lived on his faher's farm until 1850. In that year he came to Cleveland to reside with his brother, Dr. Henry Everett; attending the public school until 1853, when he entered the employ of S. Raymond & Co. In March of the succeeding year he was admitted to a clerkship in the banking house of Brockway, Wason, Everett & Co., and three years after his entrance was promoted to the position of cashier. In 1859 he was called to Philadelphia, Pa., to aid in settling up the affairs of his uncle, Charles Everett, Esq., a well known merchant who was about to retire from active business life. After a year spent in that work he returned to Cleveland and resumed his position in the banking house. In 1867, the firm having changed by the retirement of two of the partners, he became a member of the new firm of Everett, Weddell & Co. In 1869 the Republicans elected him City Treasurer by a large majority. At the end of the first year he presented to the Concil a clear, concise and complete statement of the financial affairs of the city. This had not been done for some time before. The outstanding obligations of the city were at the same time managed with such ability that the outlay for interest was largely reduced, and the credit of the city was so greatly improved that the municipal bonds were sought for by investors at a decided advance, and in many instances a premium. This improved condition of the city's financial management continuing, he was renominated at the end of his term of two years, and re-elected by a large majority. In 1873, at the end of his second term, he was nominated by both the Republican and Democratic conventions, and was again elected, receivng the largest vote that had ever been polled for one candidate from the organization of the city to that time. In 1875 and again in 1877, the same compliment was paid him, he being a third time the nominee of both parties, and elected by a unanimous vote. In 1879 he was unanimously nominated by the Republican party—the Democrats making a separate nomination. This election was hotly contested upon local issues, but he nevertheless was elected by about five thousand majority. The confidence of the public in Mr. Everett's ability as a financier, and his trustworthiness as a man, was shewn not only by his election for six consecutive terms to one of most important and responsible positions in the city government, but also by the other offices of trust to which he was chosen without his seeking. In 1876 he was elected one of the Directors and also Vice-President of the Second National Bank, one of the leading institutions of the State. He assumed management on the 1st of June, 1876, and the following year was made the President, which position he still holds. He is also Vice President and Treasurer of the VALLEY RAILWAY COMPANY, and it was largely through his influence that funds were raised for the completion of this road. He is a Director of the Cleveland Rolling Mill Co., of the Union Steel Screw Co., the Citizens' Savings and Loan Association, the Saginaw Mining Co., Lake Superior; the American District Telegraph Co., and of Everett, Weddell & Co., bankers; he is also a Director and the Treasurer of the Northern Ohio Fair Association. In January, 1880, he was unanimously appointed by the City Council one of the Sinking Fund Commissioners of the city in place of Leonard Case, deceased. All these enterprises have found him an efficient and trustworthy officer. His capacity for work is almost unlimited and his financial ability is unquestioned, while his uniform good temper, displayed in all business transactions, renders him one of the most popular of Cleveland's citizens. He is enterprising and public spirited, liberal and benevolent in regard to charitable institutions and causes, and highly esteemed in all the relations of life.

SAMUEL BRIGGS,

Superintendent of the VALLEY RAILWAY, was born in the city of New York, Aprtl 12th, 1841. His father was a merchant in that city, and was of a family originally from Rhode Island, one branch of which was established in the vicinity of New York City in 1728. Mr. Briggs was educated at the public school of the tenth ward, and at an early age was admitted into the Free Academy (now the College of the City of New York) but having a desire for a business career, completed but three years of the collegiate course, at the conclusion of which he entered the establishment of his father. After a short experience in the affairs of the house he concluded that he would try his fortune elsewhere, but failed for a long time to impress upon his father the importance of the step. The importunities of the son were finally successful, and with the prediction "he will be back in two weeks," he started for the West. After an aimless wandering for about six weeks, he finally reached Sandusky, Ohio, where by the merest accident he was ushered into his present career, entering the service of the Mad River and Lake Erie R. R. Co. (now known as the Cincinnati, Sandusky and Cleveland R. R.) From this period he bacame a railroad *nomad*, serying in the employ of various corporations in Ohio and Pennsylvania as brakeman, fireman, bill-maker, freight house forman, cashier, chief clerk, agent, etc., etc. In January, 1865, he entered the service of the A. & G. W. R. R., at Cleveland, O., and (with the exception of two years spent in the service of the Reno Shipping Co., in Penna.) has been a resident there ever since. In 1873 he was chosen Secretary of the Northern Ohio Fair Association, and served that organization creditably for seven years. He was the Secretary and Treasurer of the Euclid Avenue Opera House during its corporate existence, has been Secretary of the Masonic Temple Association since its organization in 1871, and for the past fifteen years has been personally identified with the fraternity, holding many positions of honor and trust. Politicaliy, he has had some experience; was member of the Board of Education for the fourth ward for two years, and in 1877 was honored by the Democratic convention with a nomination for the important trust of Treasurer of Cuyahoga County, and though the complexion of the district is ordinarily Republican by a majority of three thousand, Mr. Briggs was only defeated by a majority of less than three hundred. Mr. Briggs was appointed to the position he now holds on the 1st of November, 1879, and possessing good executive ability, untiring industry, unswevering devotion to the interests he is called to serve, besides the prestige of having been uniformly successful in his previous employments; there is no doubt but he will achieve additional reputation in the management of the affairs of the VALLEY RAILWAY COMPANY.

INDEX.